Sudbury Common Lands

SUDBURY COMMON LANDS

The Meadows, the Freemen and the Borough

JOHN WARDMAN

*Commemorating the first hundred years
of the
Sudbury Common Lands Charity*

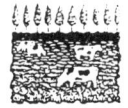

Sudbury Common Lands Charity
1996

Published 1996 by Sudbury Common Lands Charity, Longstop Cottage, The Street, Lawshall, Bury St Edmunds IP29 4QA

ISBN 0 9520812 2 9

© 1996 Sudbury Common Lands Charity and John Wardman

All rights reserved. No part of this publication may be reproduced, stored in a retrieval system, or transmitted in any form or by any means, electronic, mechanical, photocopying, recording or otherwise without the prior permission of the Sudbury Common Lands Charity.

Cover from a painting by Anne Wilding, 1990
Produced by Yard Publishing Services, Sudbury, CO10 6AG
Printed by Antony Rowe Ltd, Bumper's Farm, Chippenham, SN14 6QA

British Library Cataloguing-in-Publication Data. A catalogue entry for this book can be obtained from the British Library

CONTENTS

Foreword	7
Introduction	9
History of the lands	11
The connection with the Freemen	17
How the west was won: acquisition of the western meadows	27
Who are the Freemen?	33
The Common Lands become a charity	39
Harp Close Meadow	42
The present scheme for the charity	46
Activities on the Common Lands	48
Duties of the Trustees	53
Charitable works	59
What of the future?	62
Where to find what and when on the meadows	69
Permanent features	77
Postscript	80
Appendixes	83

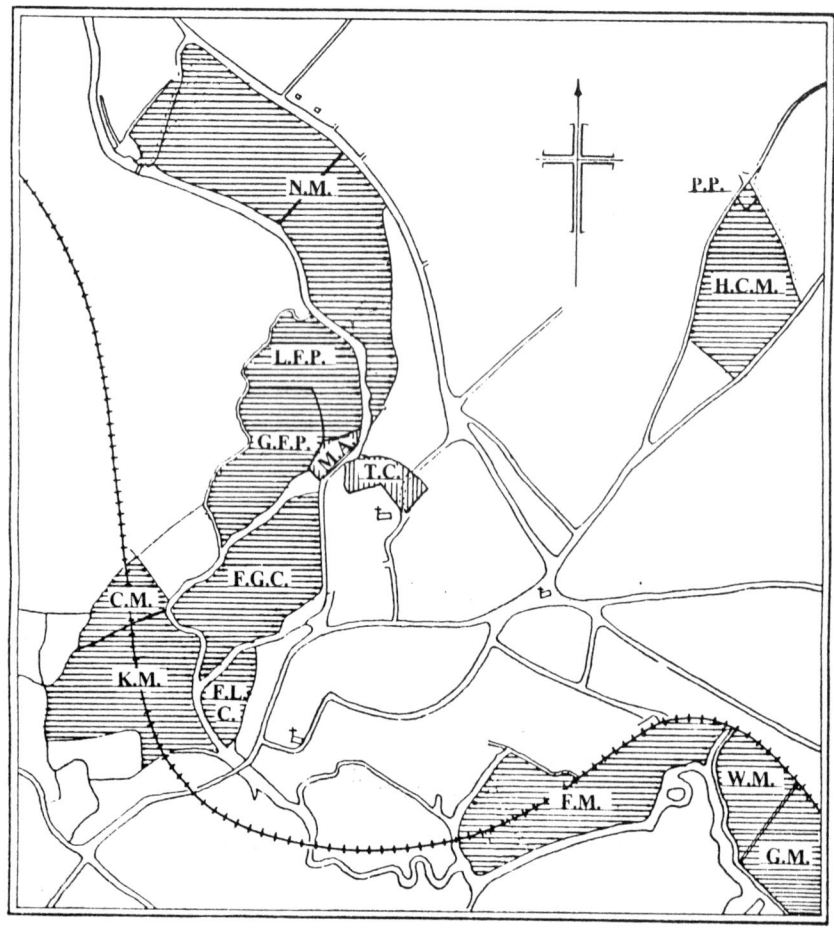

SUDBURY COMMON LANDS, PAST AND PRESENT

Based on map in History of Sudbury *by C. G. Grimwood and S. A. Kay (1952), showing the course of the river before dredging.*

N.M.	North Meadow	C.M.	Coote's Meadow
L.F.P.	Little Fulling Pit	K.M.	Kings Marsh
G.F.P.	Great Fulling Pit	P.P.	Pightle Piece**
M.A.	Mill Acre*	H.C.M.	Harp Close Meadow**
T.C.	The Croft*	F.M.	Friars Meadow***
F.G.C.	Freemen's Great Common	W.M.	Walters Meadow
F.L.C.	Freemen's Little Common	G.M.	Guilford Meadow

*Owned by Sudbury Town Council – never Common Land. **Sold to Regional Health Authority in 1987. ***Sold to Atkins Fulford/Sudbury Borough Council 1960/65

FOREWORD

This story of the Common Lands has been written for the man on a Chambers Omnibus or the lady on the Lovejoy Line, or even the youngster at school. It tries to set out the how, the why and the wherefore of these meadows in simple language. It is *not* intended as a reference book for historical scholars, though historical facts should be correct; think of it as a simplified explanation of the confused and often turbulent history of these lands.

As the story of the meadows is inextricably interwoven with the history of the town, both are mentioned, with special emphasis on the areas where one has a direct effect on the other. Similarly with the surrounding meadows; the story of the Freemen's lands cannot be divorced from the other watermeadows.

Use has been made of all sorts of sources. I am particularly indebted to Alan Berry for his resumé of the history of the Common Lands and permission to make use of his many books. I have also made extensive use of a synopsis of the original deeds as compiled by Miles Braithwaite in 1911, the *History of Sudbury* (1952) by C. G. Grimwood and S. A. Kay, Phyllis Felton's collection of material on the Walnuttree Hospital and St Gregory's church, the Sudbury Town Archives, and the Minute Books of the Common Lands Charity. In addition, specialist information on the flora and fauna has been supplied by Adrian Walters, the Clerk/Ranger to the Charity. Many other people have helped in various ways, including Sam Thornton who rooted out ancient maps, old friends with their reminiscences, a senior executive of the Rivers Authority, and the superior knowledge of many Trustees of the Charity. To all these I give my thanks.

A few definitions would be useful before starting to read.

Shackage is the practice of turning animals on to field, after the crop has been gathered, to feed off the stubble, fallen grain and other residue – fields used to be full of weeds. *Shackage rights* are the rights of persons not owning the land to do this with their animals. It was normally restricted to the winter months, from old St Bartholomew's

FOREWORD

Day to Candlemas, when no grass was growing on the meadows. Such land was known as *half-yearly* land.

Pasturage is the herbage for cattle. Thus the right to pasturage allows a third party to depasture beasts on meadows he does not own. Sometimes this right was only available after a hay crop had been cut. The residue in this case was known as the *aftermath*; the locally accepted date for turning on for this was August 15th.

John Wardman
June 1996

'View of Sudbury from the South-East', colour aquatint and etching by James Scales, c. 1821. Reproduced by kind permission of Gainsborough's House, Sudbury.
Photo by Curtis Lane & Co., Sudbury

Here Sudbury is viewed across Allens brickfield, showing the Quay right centre, with the two windmills at the top of North Street behind. Ballingdon Bridge is to the extreme left and Friars Meadow is to the right with Belle Vue on the skyline beyond.

INTRODUCTION

This booklet has been prepared to commemorate the first hundred years of the Sudbury Common Lands Charity. The first sections trace the history of the land, the role of the Freemen, and the formation of the Charity itself. The latter sections detail the activities of the Charity from its formation to the present day. Ancient laws and customs have been explained so that the history of these ancient pastures can be more readily appreciated.

The land came under the jurisdiction of the Common Lands Charity in 1897 as the result of a High Court case between the Freemen and the Borough Council. Prior to this the Council had administered the land on behalf of the Freemen.

The Scheme setting up the Charity described the land to be vested in the Charity Commission and administered by the Trustees thus:

Description of land	A.	R.	P.
Harp Close Meadow	16	0	0
* Part of Common	10	0	27
Great and Little Fulling Pit Meadow	24	1	0
North Meadow	41	1	0
Friars Meadow	22	0	20
* Part of Commons	12	1	23
** Ballingdon Marshes	19	0	34
Total	145	1	24

* *Now known as Freemen's Great & Little Common. When the Freemen were given the land in about 1262 it was known as Portmannescroft.*
** *Now known as Kings Marsh; Kingsmere in 1262.*
A.R.P. stands for Acres (about 0.4 Hectares), Roods (quarter of an Acre) and Perches (30 1/4 square yards or 1/160 Acres)

Since the Charity was formed the Trustees have sold some of this land and obtained other meadows. These changes are listed elsewhere in the book.

All these lands are shown on the map on page 6, and form a great

INTRODUCTION

arc round the town following the course of the River Stour. As a matter of interest the local pronunciation is Stower (two syllables), an ancient way of spelling it. At Manningtree they rhyme it with 'your' and further inland it rhymes with 'our'. Apart from Harp Close Meadow, which was acquired *c.* 1876 as high-level grazing, all the meadows were liable to flooding each year.

'View of Sudbury from the south-east', c. 1860, by Henry Bridgman (1831–1909). Now in Gainsborough's House, Sudbury. Reproduced by kind permission. Photo by Curtis Lane & Co., Sudbury, Suffolk

Guilford Meadow is shown left foreground, Walters Meadow in middle of picture, and Friars Meadow across the bridge along the townscape. The newly built railway line is shown in the picture, terminating just near the junction of Cornard Road and Great Eastern Road.

HISTORY OF THE LANDS

The next few pages give a brief outline of how the meadows evolved from a marshy wooded area to the pastures we know today.

Though mammoth teeth have been found in workings on the meadows — larger portions have been found nearby – it cannot be assumed that such giant creatures roamed over these grounds, though they probably did; the remains could easily have been transported here from elsewhere during the last Ice Age.

At some stage, after the glaciers had receded, all the present meadows were marshy and wooded with the river running through. The meandering watercourse, weaving and snaking its way towards the sea, would have carved out the Stour Valley to its present width. The river bed moved over the years; sometimes it may have occupied more than one channel. Floods would have broken through the banks. Silt, brought down from further upstream, would be spread over the whole area. Islands would form only to vanish after a decade or two, rushes would clog the water courses, trees would grow and then get washed away; it was an ever-changing scene.

As soon as man came to settle he would have gathered reeds and wood to form shelters and to provide fuel for his fires. When all the fallen timber was used he started to fell trees. This changed the landscape and represented the first land management, haphazard though it was. After some time the treeless marshy areas would have become suitable for use as pasture for grazing his stock. The next obvious task was to increase the area by digging drainage ditches; these would also delineate the boundaries and help to establish ownership. Drainage improved the quality of the grass and let the stock graze for longer periods.

We know that cattle have grazed these pastures continually for at least the last nine hundred years. Not only cattle. In medieval times St John's Hospital, sited just north of Ballingdon Bridge, was granted the right to graze four cows and twenty sheep on part of the land. In the reign of James I (1603–1625) hogs were banned; presumably they had been grazing there before this date. Horses have fed on the rich grass; in fact, out of 180 grazing beasts in 1729, only 53 were cows.

All have contributed to make the sward as it is today. This was done in two ways. First, cropping removed tree seedlings and kept the coarser, stronger grasses at bay letting the finer species multiply. Second, the droppings acted as a natural fertiliser. Wild geese and rabbits made their smaller contributions in a similar way, though it was only recently, historically speaking, that rabbits discovered that they could survive and multiply outside man-managed warrens! More recently some feral geese dumped on the meadows caused problems. Like goats, geese crop very close to the ground and seem to have a particular taste for lady's smock (cuckooflower); they decimated the stocks of this attractive wildflower that had been encouraged to grow over the previous years. Since the geese were humanely removed to a better home this plant has flourished.

Animals were not alone in fertilising the grassland. The floods used to deposit a rich silt of decayed vegetable matter from further upstream on to the land. In recent years this previously welcome addition to fertility has become a problem with the leaching of nitrates and phosphates from arable farmland, causing a noticeable change in the type of grasses that flourish.

In the distant past the effluent draining from the sewers through streams and ditches into the river also had a beneficial effect on the richness of the pasture. As with the nitrates, this became too much of a good thing. When the population expanded so did the outflow from the sewers. A couple of centuries ago the river was so polluted by these discharges that the Mayor, who as the most senior Freeman claimed the right to all the fish in the Stour, found that, like St Peter, his nets were empty.

A further source of pollution in earlier days was that caused by the practice of processing freshly woven cloth on the meadows. Before work on the cloth could start, a cart would be sent round the town for the express purpose of purchasing the contents of piss-pots at a penny a go. The urine was then used to bleach the cloth, while the clay dug from the meadows was used to *full* the woven material. This process made the cloth thicker, in the same way that textiles are dressed today. Not only did Fulling Pit Meadow get its name from this process – the pit where the fulling took place – but the *clay*, native hydrated aluminium silicate, became known as fuller's earth. Today this kaolin-like substance is used in filtration plants and as a dusting powder; traces of the remains of the pits from where it was dug can still be seen.

It is probable that the undulating area towards the river opposite the Mill Hotel is a result of the digging of earth to repair the mill-pool; Elizabeth de Burgh reserved this right in her charter of 1330. More recently the Mill Hotel availed itself of the same inherited right; unlike Elizabeth its owners used mechanical diggers.

The most likely reason for the present pattern of the water courses was the decision to build a water mill, probably on the site of the present Mill Hotel. The first mentioned was in the Domesday Book of 1086; like nearly all the other mills in the country it was entered in the records because mills were then an important source of revenue – a taxable asset. Brundon Mill was also listed: 'Brundon ... wood for twenty swine, twenty-two acres of meadowland, and one mill'.

How and when all the changes took place it is impossible to determine, though it is probable that the overflow from the floodgates was cut in Anglo-Saxon times.

A map of the meadows today shows two distinct islands. Freemen's Great and Little Common have been combined to form one; to the north, Great and Little Fulling Pit Meadow form the other.

Until 1955 the Great and Little Commons were separated by the river flowing from the Mill Pool to a point near where the bridge crosses into Kings Marsh – the footings of a demolished bridge crossing this vanished waterway are still visible to the careful observer!

About the same time the Essex River Board started major river works to reduce the severity of the regular flooding. The Stour between Cornard Mill and Lady's Bridge was straightened to such an extent that Lady's Island was formed, meanders between Friars Meadow and the railway bridge were removed, the river was considerably widened on Freemen's Little Common, and the Salmon Jump was made. To celebrate this the river was stocked with salmon. This part of the experiment did little more than move the junction with the Pike Ditch about ten yards up-stream to its present position – as far as is known, no mature salmon have been caught in this stretch of the Stour.

The river has been dredged frequently over the years. Evidence of this can be seen by the *levees* on both banks of the river, particularly on the portion between the Salmon Jump and the Old Bathing Place. It is possible that the natural river followed this course until it ran round the back of Mill Acre via Berry's Ditch. The thinking behind this supposition is that no one in their right mind would create such a wide watercourse to feed the mill when a much narrower one, like the one from the Croft to the Mill, would have sufficed. This latter section of the Mill Lade is definitely man-made – the water level is so much higher than the adjacent meadowland.

Water level is controlled by dams, weirs and sluices. The Salmon Jump includes a weir while the floodgates are a good example of a sluice. This latter used to be controlled by a *lock-keeper* who lived in a cottage just by the sluice on the site now known as Mill Acre. This piece of land was mentioned in documents dated 1731 but has never been part of the Common Lands. At present it is owned by Sudbury Town Council.

Having got the water to the mill, channels had to be dug to return all the diverted water back to the main river. The present course is via what is little more than a ditch running behind the gardens of the houses in Cross Street though, as mentioned earlier, this has only recently become the sole route.

The last major change to affect the meadows was the construction of the railway line from Sudbury to Melford in 1865–67. The line crossed over two separate areas of Freemen's land.

One section ran across Friars Meadow from near the new station to the bridge over the canal that runs up to the Quay. This cut off the area round Atkins Fulford factory from the rest of the meadows. The present railway station is the third that has served Sudbury. The first, when the Borough was the terminus of the Marks Tey branch line, was built on land now forming part of the goods delivery entrance to the Solar supermarket near the junction of Great Eastern Road and Cornard Road. The second was at the end of Station Approach covering much of the present station car park and stretching to behind the Kingfisher Pool.

The second section of line over the commons, starting near the site of the former Ballingdon pumping station and running towards Brundon Mill, effectively cut King's Marsh into two.

The Great Eastern Railway, later the London and North Eastern Railway, bought from the Freemen the strip of land across Kings Marsh to build their track. The money was invested under the authority of the Court of Chancery and was later used in part payment for Harp Close Meadow.

Bathing used to take place officially in a deeper part of the river just downstream of the point where the Pike Ditch joins the watercourse flowing from the floodgate pool. The bathing place has been known as Dobbs Hole, although there is another 'Dobbs Hole' in the town. In 1894 a proper bathing place was constructed about 150 yards upstream from the Croft Bridge. To gain access from Fulling Pit Meadow a second bridge had to be constructed to get the prospective swimmers across to the changing booths and shallow area; the original bridge was replaced in the early 1930s. A route from Melford Road was provided by means of a new footpath for customers from that side of town. A licence fee was paid to the Freemen by the Borough Council so that this path could never become a public right of way; this fee is still paid today! Chestnut trees were planted to soften the outline of the buildings. Mixed bathing was forbidden, and canvas screens were erected to prevent the local lads on the meadows gazing on the ladies as they besported themselves in the water. This facility was closed in 1936 following a health scare, and a grand new bathing pool was built at the southern end of Newton Road, just behind the site of the old Police Station, and formally opened in June 1939.

A few other oddities are worth recording, not all strictly to do with the Common Lands.

Around 1940 a seaplane attempted to land on the Reach on Friars Meadows. It was piloted by a Dutchman escaping from the Nazi occupation. It was not totally successful, as the plane crashed in Ballingdon Grove, but the pilot survived.

To thwart an airborne invasion tall poles were planted on all the riverside meadows. These were spaced closer together than the wing-span of the German gliders to prevent them from landing.

About ten pill-boxes were constructed along the natural defence line formed by the river between Cornard Mill and Brundon Mill. All were on the Essex bank – all foot-bridges were removed – thus Sudbury was not an option for the defenders' line of retreat. Quite rightly, too, as the line of defence was against invaders, having landed in Suffolk or Norfolk, reaching London.

The previous paragraphs are intended to show how the meadows have been shaped by management and other factors over the centuries; future management by the Trustees will continue to play an important part in the life of these pastures. Without management they would become truly wild areas, unattractive to both man and his beasts. Over-intensive management would turn them into a sterile town park with gravel paths, mown grass and manicured hedges.

The aim of the Trustees is to implement a management scheme to the benefit of the townspeople, the Freemen, the cattle and the wildlife, a considerable task, and one that can only be successful with the advice and assistance from English Nature, Babergh District Council, Dedham Vale Project, the Ministry of Agriculture and Fisheries Project Officer and our highly qualified Ranger with the Five-Year Management Plan members. Plus, of course, the support of the citizens of Sudbury.

THE CONNECTION WITH THE FREEMEN

How did the Freemen acquire the various fields and meadows that are now known as the Common Lands?

In Anglo-Saxon times individual Freemen had certain rights and privileges. One of these was the right to depasture beasts on specified meadows between certain dates without owning the land. Some of these pastures may have been communally owned but most would have been part of a farmstead or manor, with the Freemen having grazing rights for about six months of the year – during the period the grass was growing. In the winter they had to find other accommodation for their beasts. They used land up from the valley floor, dryer land, land that was farmed. These fields were known as half-yearly land, and the Freemen enjoyed rights of shackage there. The Freemen had *rights in common* over these different types of land; this meant that no individual Freeman had special rights over a particular piece of land; all the rights belonged equally to all the Freemen.

Thus, in this case the words *Common Lands* indicate lands over which each Freeman has rights in common with all other Freemen in the same way that two or three householders have common rights over a shared drive owned by a landlord; it does *not* mean, as is often claimed and is sometimes the case elsewhere, that the lands belong to the commonalty – *the common people*. A quotation from *Essential Law for Landowners and Farmers* puts the position succinctly. 'Many people think that common land is owned by the people at large, and that they are entitled to wander over it. In fact, common land is usually owned by private individuals, or by bodies such as the National Trust or the Church Commissioners. However it is subject to rights exercised by third parties, that is, the commoners'. In this case the commoners, those who have the rights in common, are the Freemen. There are over 8,500 commons in England. The majority of these are privately owned

LAND ACQUISITIONS AND SALES LISTED IN CHRONOLOGICAL ORDER

Date	From	Meadow	Acres	Cost
1262	Richard de Clare	Meadow	18.	} £5 plus
1262	Richard de Clare	Freemen's Gt Common (F.G.C.)	4.5	} £2 p.a.
1262	Richard de Clare	Freemen's Lt Common (F.L.C.)	19.2	
1731	John Knight	Lt. Fulling Pit (Part (L.F.P.)	8.	5/-
??	John Taylor	Lt. Fulling Pit (Rest) (L.F.P.)	2.45	??
1841	Goody, Stedman, King, Oliver (Shackage)	North Meadow (N.M.5)	8.7	Exchng
1844	T.&J. Jones (Shackage)	North Meadow (N.M.9)	3.9	Exchng
1846	Paving Commissioners	North Meadow (N.M.6)	2.5	£202
1849	T. Jones (Shackage)	North Meadow (N.M.7)	2.5	Exchng
1850	T. Jones (Shackage)	North Meadow (N.M.8)	2.1	Exchng
1862	Mortan, Skipworth, Morant (Shackage)	North Meadow (N.M.4)	20.	*£1360
1862	Mortan, Skipworth, Morant (Shackage)	Gt Fulling Pit (G.F.P)	13.8	*4£940
1875	Argent (Shackage)	Pightle Piece (P.P.)	0.7	Exchng
1876	Grover	Harp Close Meadow (H.C.M.)	15.3	**£1628
1895	S.M.C. (Colney)	North Meadow (N.M.1)	2.9	Exchng
Total			124.55	
1945-1959	Various	§Friars' Meadow (F.M.)	22.1	???

§ *Included in the 1897 Scheme though Freemen had only the right to feed off the aftermath. Most purchased in 1945; F.M.1 & 2 were not bought until 1955/59 from two local charities.*

	Total acreage according to deeds etc. in 1897	146.42
	Total acreage according to the 1897 Scheme	145.4

Subsequent purchases/sales by the Trustees

1901	Weybrew (Shackage)	North Meadow (N.M.2)	1.0	} £7.54
1901	Weybrew (Shackage)	North Meadow (N.M.3)	0.9	
1959	Armsey Farm (?)	Coote's Meadow	4.7	£ 125.00
1960	To: Atkins Fulford	Friars Meadow (F.M.(a))	5.3	(£5000)
1965	To: Sudbury B.C.	Friars Meadow (F.M.(b))	16.8	(£3000)
1987	To: Hospital Authority	Harp Close Meadow (P.P & H.C.M.)	16.	(£850000)
1994	Stephen Walters Ltd	Walters Meadow (W.M.)	6.6	Leased
1995	Guilford Europe	Guilford Meadow (G.M.)	12.5	Leased
Total 1997			134.12	

* *Purchased with money from sale of land to G.E.R. for railway.*
** *Purchased with money obtained from the release of shackage at Woodhall.*

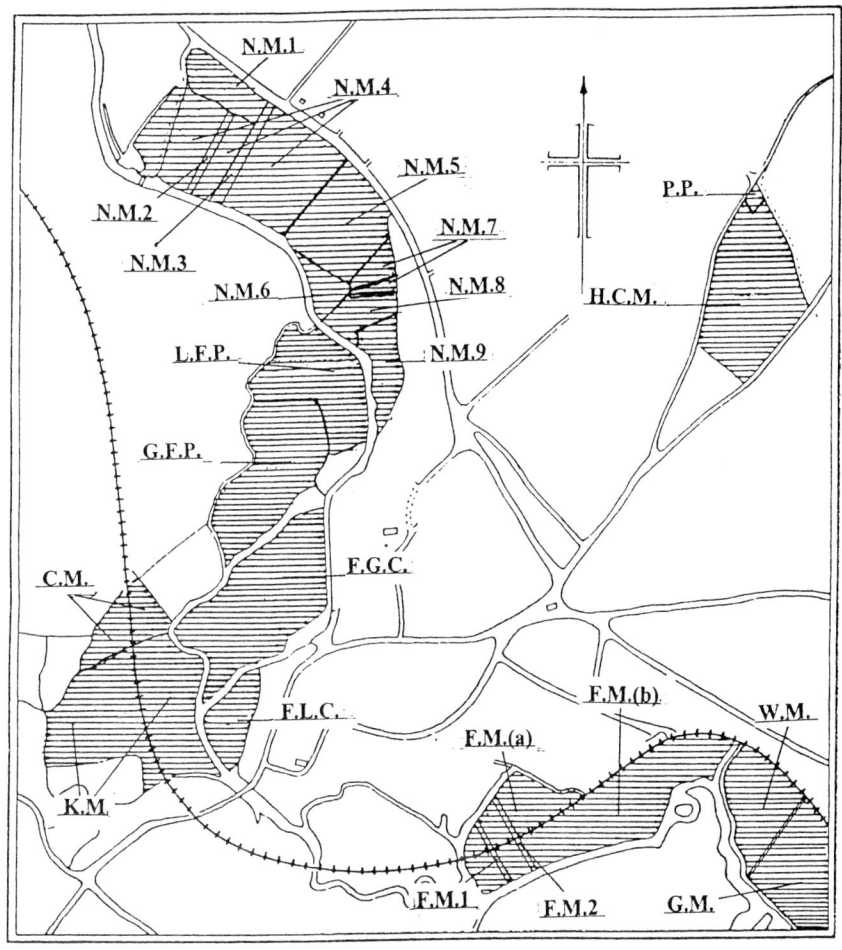

Lands acquired by gift and purchase. (Based on map used by Grimwood and Kay)

In the Middle Ages land was most frequently cultivated in strips. To prevent the lands' becoming exhausted (remember artificial fertilizers were not available), different crops would be grown on a strip on successive years; some years the ground would be left fallow - the forerunner of 'set-aside'! These strips, or 'doles', were owned individually. Sometimes a richer farmer would buy several strips, enlarging his property; but over the years isolated doles were left in the middle of large fields. Examples of this can be seen on the map, viz. N.M.2, N.M.3, F.M.1 and F.M.2.

and on only about 1,700 are the general public allowed access! Though the public has no 'rights' to leave the designated footpaths, it is the intention of the Trustees to continue to allow the public access over most of the lands under their control, where practical.

In other areas in England rights of common can include the collection of wood, the grazing of pigs or ponies, the cutting of peat turves or the mining for coal, but only by those who have the necessary qualifications. In such places, those with this privilege have it by virtue of owning a specific house or living in a certain restricted area, by descent, or by some similar qualification.

After the Norman Conquest Sudburgh (Sudbury), previously a Saxon manor, became a Royal manor, as did most of the other burghs in the country.

William the Conqueror repaid his Norman knights by giving them land in return for pledges of service and loyalty (and in so doing introduced feudalism into England); the de Clare family were recipients of the lordship of the Manor of Sudbury. A direct descendant, one Richard de Clare, Earl of Gloucester and Hertford, then one of the most important Lords in the Kingdom, *gave* the first of our Common Lands to the Freemen by a charter in about 1262. This document stipulated that it was 'to be had and held by the said burgesses and their successors quietly, wholly, rightly, peaceably, and by inheritance .... for ever against all people.' The land in question then became Freemen's Common Lands.

The expression that he *gave* the land to the Burgesses, or 'Freemen' as they are known today, needs explanation. The word *leased* would have been a more appropriate description, as the Freemen were required to pay 100 shillings as a down payment plus 40 silver shillings a year. This was not the bargain it seemed, for the Freemen gained little that they had not enjoyed as a right for many years; their main benefit was that the charter showed in writing that they had a good title to the land. The most likely reason that Richard de Clare *gave* these lands was that he needed to improve his fortunes, depleted by an extravagant life-style, by realising some of his assets.

These first lands consisted of Portsmannescroft and Kingsmere; the

THE CONNECTION WITH THE FREEMEN

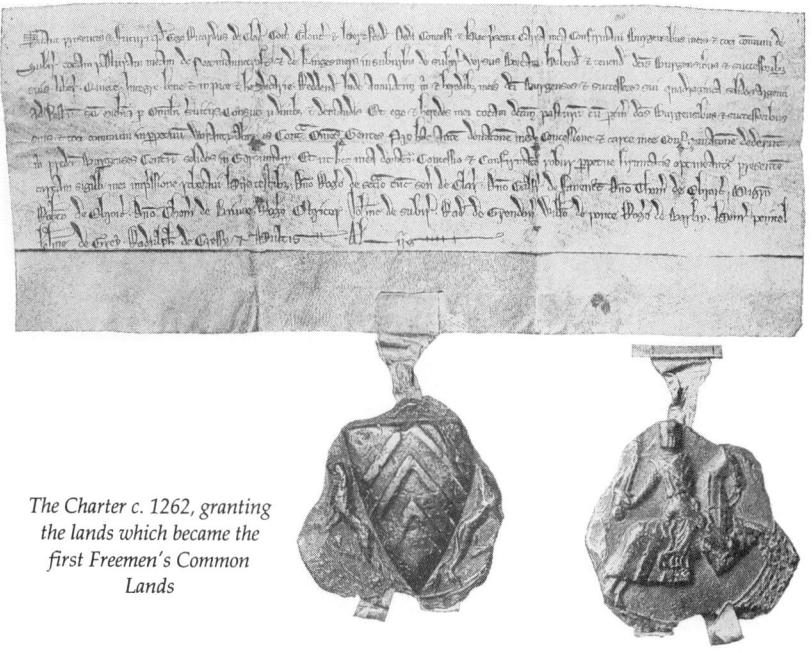

The Charter c. 1262, granting the lands which became the first Freemen's Common Lands

name Portsmannescroft shows the connection with the Freemen prior to this date. Portman = Burgess = Freeman, therefore Portmannescroft = Freeman's Croft = Freeman's Common. The Freemen paid their dues to the Earl until the Earldom became extinct in 1314, and then to a female descendant, Elizabeth de Burgh, the Lady of Clare (founder of Clare College, Cambridge), and subsequently to her heirs until at least 1425, but possibly until the mid 18th century, a total of 500 years.

The rights of the Freemen to these pastures and to the *free* fishing were confirmed by Queen Mary in 1554 and by Queen Elizabeth in 1559; the 'free' fishing cost 6s. 8d. (33.3p) a year.

The next land acquired by the Freemen to graze their cattle was a 14-acre pasture called Armsey, in Bulmer. It was given to the Freemen in the middle of the fifteenth century by Thomas West, probably a Freeman himself and a Mayor of Sudbury. It seems the Freemen had only half-yearly grazing rights in spite of it being gifted to them; this was quite normal farming procedure. This upland pasture was sold in

1839 for £1,200 and the money used to purchase other land for the Freemen. A strip forty-three feet wide had to be left by the new owner for the main road south and footpaths; the present Halstead Road, where it passes Armsey Farm, was once Freemen's Land.

The first section of Fulling Pit Meadow, some eight acres known as Earles Meadow, was bought by the Freemen from John Knight, of Gosfield Hall, in 1731. The indenture conveys the land to certain named Freemen (the Mayor, Aldermen and Chief Burgesses of the Borough) and states that the land is 'for the use, benefit and advantage ... of all and every other the freemen who are or who shall hereafter be free of the Common belonging to the said Borough for ever.' This style of conveyance was used in all similar documents for the land administered by Sudbury Common Lands Charity until 1897, i.e. it was written in favour of the Mayor, Aldermen and Burgesses for the benefit of the Freemen.

In 1838 Parliament passed the Sudbury Town Lands Act. This legislation allowed landowners to redeem shackage rights by giving Freemen land in exchange, often with a cash adjustment. The importance of this Act was that it enabled the Freemen to have a good title to the land they thus obtained, as good a title as any other land purchased freehold.

The Freemen, in these times, had the right of depasturing over much of the Bartholomew and Woodhall estates. By redeeming these lands the farmers were able to grow root crops on what had been half-yearly land, instead of having to leave them fallow for the six months that the Freemen's cattle would have been on them. The Meadows could only be grazed in the summer months when the grass was growing; if the cattle were left on during the winter the sward would be too closely cropped and the hooves of the beasts would turn it into a quagmire. Hence they were kept on dryer ground in the winter where they fed off the stubble of the farmers crop and feed brought in by their owners. The farmers were repaid by the fertiliser the cows left behind them; there were no concentrates in those days. As all these fields were near to the town, redemption of the shackage rights allowed the owners to sell the land for building houses, schools and hospitals, a profitable transaction for farmers then as it is now.

In 1841 the first parcel of land obtained by the Freemen under this scheme was a section of North Meadow – four different landowners conveyed a total of just over eight acres lying on either side of the footpath running from Melford Road to Brundon Mill.

In 1844 nearly four acres behind the Old Bathing Place were obtained by the same method. Further portions of North Meadow were conveyed to the Freemen in 1846, 1849, 1850 and 1862, some as redemption of shackage, some as normal sales. Except for two tiny strips handed over in 1901, the final portion of North Meadow, at the junction of Melford Road and Brundon Lane, was conveyed from the Colney Charity Trustees to the Freemen in 1895. This was the vineyard left by John Colney, himself a leper, in 1372 as part of an endowment to provide a leper hospital on the site of Colney Close. This was known as St Leonard's and the income from the Colney Charity helped to build a new St Leonard's Hospital in Newton Road in 1868.

Apart from the acquisition of part of North Meadow, 1862 was also the date that the whole of Great Fulling Pit was purchased by a combination of cash and redemption.

The 1862 and 1895 redemptions released from shackage lands of the Woodhall Estate and Colney Charity; this facilitated the development of all the land from St Bartholomew's Lane to Cornard Road. A map of 1714 shows few houses outside the town centre, none on Melford Road, only a few in East Street, and clusters at the King Street end of Newton Road and Cornard Road!

All the lands owned by the Freemen up to 1875 were lands that they had previously grazed; they were also lands that were liable to winter flooding. Having disposed of so much of their half-yearly land, some high-level grazing was needed; the practice of feeding off the verges, and leaving heaps of muck there, had been severely restricted by the Paving and Lighting Act of 1825 which prohibited such goings on within eighty feet of the centre of the road. The Freemen had money in hand from the sale of land for the railway and from the redemption of shackage on Woodhall to buy a suitable field.

In 1875 Stephen Argent offered Pigtail (or Pightle) Piece to release other land from shackage and commonage. ('Pightle', pronounced pie-tle, means a small field or enclosure; a close or croft.) Pightle was probably corrupted to 'People' as Infanta de Castilla was changed to Elephant and Castle by the Cockneys, hence the transition to Pieple's Piece and then People's Park. This was just under one acre, situated in the north-west corner of Harp Close Meadow. A year later the remaining fifteen acres were offered as redemption land and were bought for £1628 11s. 3d.; this allowed the redeemed land, Newmans Piece, to be metamorphosed into Newmans Road.

Like the Western Meadows, Friars Meadow had been grazed by the cattle of Sudbury Freemen since time immemorial. The land itself was divided into strips, or *doles*, belonging to different owners, with the Freemen having the right of grazing on the aftermath after a hay crop had been gathered. This was slightly different to the situation on North Meadow where they had a longer period for grazing. In spite of the Freemen only *part-owning* the meadow, in 1897 the High Court in Chancery ruled that the title be vested in the Charity Commission and administered by the Common Lands Charity on behalf of the Freemen. This the Charity did.

In 1945 the Trustees purchased outright the greater part of the Meadow; a number of doles were aggregated and bought *en bloc*. An outstanding dole of just over an acre was purchased from the John Fenn Charity in 1956 and the last strip of just over half an acre from the Susan Girling and Robert Upcher Charity in 1959.

Over the years the western block of the Common Lands had come under increasing pressure as a recreational area, and it was this area that had the greatest historical significance for the Trustees; it was the area they least wanted to be developed in any respect. The Borough had been interested in buying Harp Close Meadow as a building site or sports field on and off for thirty years since 1944 but, for one reason or another, these applications came to nothing.

A perfect solution was found in 1961, when the Trustees rented, and later sold for a few peppercorns, almost the whole of Friars Meadow to the Borough as a sports field, while the corner cut off by the railway was sold at an economic figure to the Atkins Fulford Company as a factory site. The Council had originally wanted to use all the land as a rubbish dump in preparation for utilising it for light industry – this in 1952! Thus the Borough had its sports field, the Trustees had at least some capital, and the Western Meadows had a reprieve.

The last area of land bought by the Trustees was Coote's Meadow, nearly five acres split into two by the railway, purchased for £145 in 1959 after being rented for forty years. It is the field just north of Kings Marsh, the two halves being connected by a right of way over the railway. It had been known as Bulmer Meadow, with possible connections with Armsey.

Since the disposal of Harp Close Meadow (see chapter on Harp Close Meadow below, page 42) the Trustees have been looking, in compliance with the 1987 Scheme, to replace the land lost to grazing by this sale. Various meadowlands in the flood plain of the Stour have been looked at, but without any purchase so far.

A strip of land, consisting of three meadows, lies on the Suffolk bank of the Stour between Lady's Island and Cornard Mill. Grazing had taken place on some parts of these lands until the 1950s, though not by Freemen. They were also used at various times as playing fields; there was at least one pavilion built there. Hard by Doe's railway crossing were osier-beds where willows were grown for basket making – traces of the workshop where the osier practised his craft can still be seen. Latterly this area was given over to the growing of bat-willows or left to become untamed scrub. A railway line ran to a basin near Lady's Bridge to facilitate the loading and unloading of barges using the river.

In 1994/1995 the Trustees were able to lease two of these fields, Walters and Guilford Meadows, and started to rehabilitate them with the aid of Suffolk Wildlife Trust, Babergh District Council and English Nature, utilising grants from the Ministry of Agriculture and Fisheries.

1995, too, saw the introduction of a Ranger Service by the Common Lands Ranger over Friars Meadow, since local government reorganisation owned by Babergh District Council. This is in addition to a similar service provided to B.D.C. for Kone Vale and the Valley Walk and to the Town Council for the Croft and Mill Acre, and to the

Mill Hotel for the path from the floodgates.

One other portion of land is owned by the Charity, and that is the wooded area to the north-west of Brundon Lane between Brundon Mill and Melford Road. This was part of North Meadow and used to be grazing land but was planted with trees to commemorate the Coronation of Queen Elizabeth II.

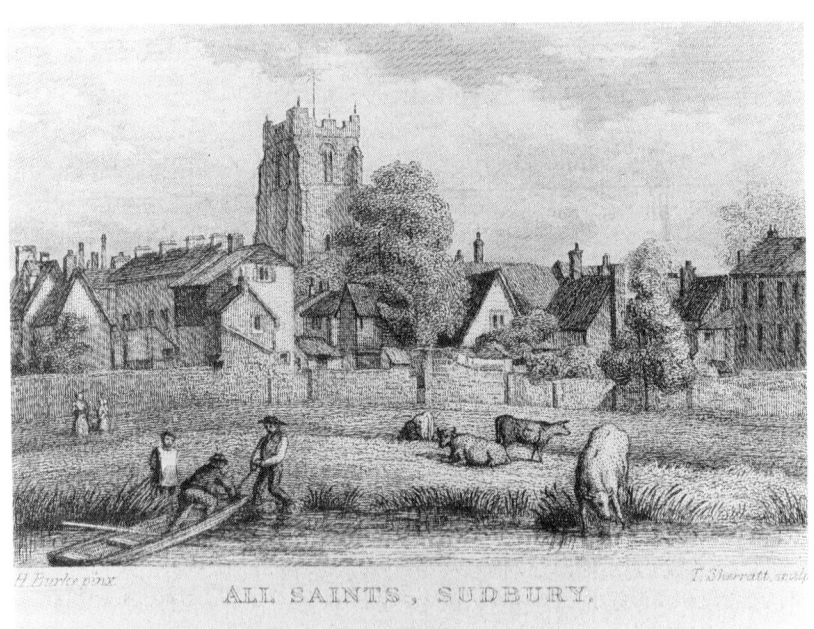

'All Saints, Sudbury', engraving by Thomas Sherratt after H. Burke. Reproduced by kind permission of Gainsborough's House, Sudbury.
Photo by Curtis Lane & Co, Sudbury

View across the river from Kings Marsh showing part of Freemen's Great Common in the foreground and Freemen's Little Common beyond the old course of the outflow from the Mill pool. The gate to Noah's Ark Lane is right of centre..

HOW THE WEST WAS WON: ACQUISITION OF THE WESTERN MEADOWS

Details of how the various parcels of land to the west of the town became Freemen's Lands over a seven hundred year period make a fascinating story and deserve to be looked at in more detail.

The first lands were given by Richard of Clare, Earl of Gloucester and Hertford, in about 1262. This transaction is well documented; the original charter, given to the Freemen, is held by the Trustees of the Common Lands and kept in the Suffolk Records Office. This document was corroborated about seventy years later by a second charter from a descendant, Elizabeth de Burgh, Lady of Clare, in terms similar to the first. In both documents the lands are described as '... all my pasture of Portmannescroft (Portmanscroft) and of Kingsmere (Kingsmarsh) in the suburb of Sudbury...'. The spelling varies between the two documents, that of the second charter being given in parentheses.

The area of the meadows is not stated in these deeds, but the 1897 Scheme gives Freemen's Great Common as 18 acres and Freemen's Little Common as 4.5 acres, while the same reference gives Kings Marsh as 19.2 acres, a total of nearly 42 acres. This closely matches the Domesday Book entry, about 175 years before the first charter, of 9 acres held by the Burgesses and 35 acres held by St Gregory's Church. As this entry is immediately followed by a reference to a mill the probability is that all these documents refer to the same pieces of land. The Cor Brewer map of 1714 confirms this, with an acreage of just over 43.

In this area, before Norman times, a Burgess of a market town (port) was known as a Portman, hence an enclosed piece of meadow (croft) over which he had rights could be termed Portmanscroft. In Ipswich the Freemen had the right to graze horses on Portman Marshes, hence the origin of the name Portman Road leading to the football ground.

HOW THE WEST WAS WON: ACQUISITION OF THE WESTERN MEADOWS

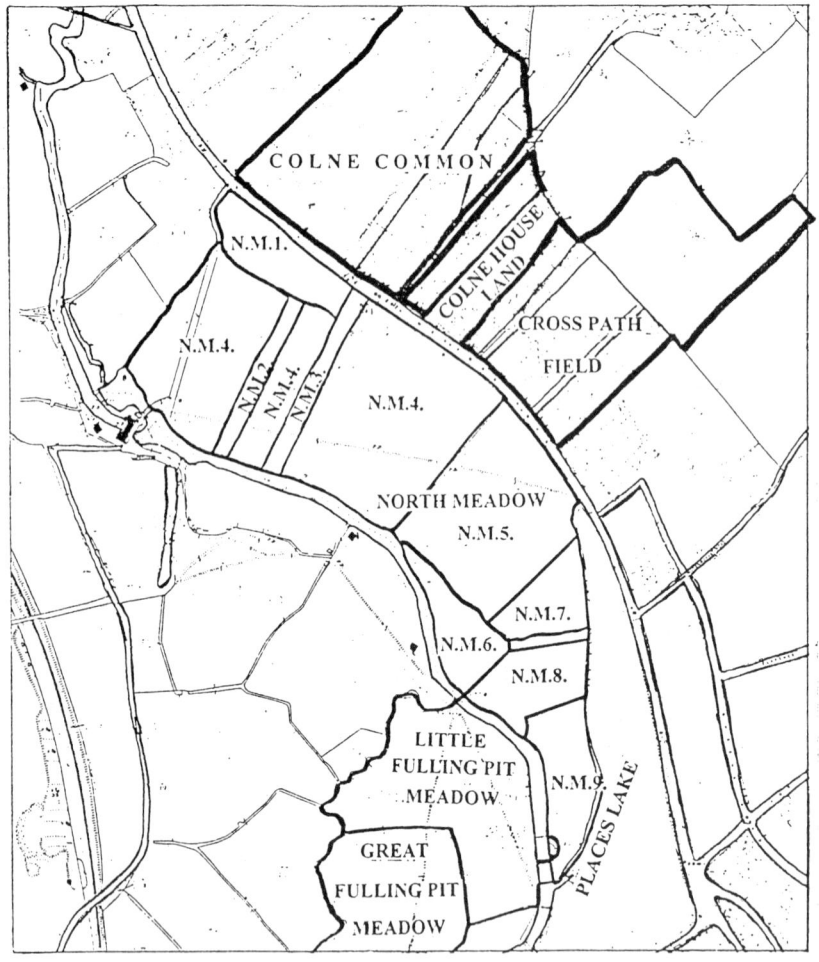

North Meadow and surrounding land

1. Land bequeathed by John Colney in 1372 to endow St Leonard's Leper Hospital, consisting of Colne House land (site of the hospital), Colney Vineyard (N.M.1), and Colne Common (shackage land not redeemed until 1925)
2. Cross Path Field and adjoining land, released from shackage in exchange for N.M.2 and N.M.3.
3. Places Lake, shown on deeds of 1844, significance unknown.

Records show that the present Freemen's Commons were known as Portmanscroft for at least seventy years, and probably very much longer, before they were given to the Freemen by Richard de Clare. Following from this and other evidence it seems logical that most, if not all, of the present Western Meadows were grazed by Freemen's cattle as of right from well before the Normans invaded.

The next of the present meadows was not obtained by the Freemen until over four hundred and fifty years later, on 23 September 1731, though they had exercised their right of grazing over it for many years before. These eight acres were called Earles Meadow, otherwise Fulling Pit Meadow, and were sold by John Knight Esquire of Gosfield to the Mayor and Burgesses for the 'use, benefit and advantage of themselves and of all and every other the freemen who are or shall hereafter be free of the Common belonging to the said Borough for ever'. Five shillings was paid for this meadow bounded by the river to the east, a meadow belonging to the Manor of Woodhall to the west, to the north a meadow owned by John Taylor and to the south a piece of meadow called Mill Acre. It is now called Little Fulling Pit Meadow. The remaining two and a half acres were acquired subsequently from John Taylor, though details of the transaction are not known. The five shillings paid was probably a peppercorn rent whereby a nominal lease was converted the next day into a release giving possession. John Knight had bought this land for five shillings ten years before, then paid £182.50 the next day for the release.

The Sudbury Town Lands Act was passed by Parliament in 1838. This, as mentioned earlier, allowed the Freemen and landowners to exchange grazing rights for land, with or without a cash adjustment either way. Armsey in Bulmer, acquired by the Freemen in the first half of the fifteenth century from St Gregory's College, was the first piece of land to be sold by them under this act.

The first portion of land obtained under the new legislation, N.M.5 on the map, was eight acres, two roods and thirty-seven perches of North Meadow from John Crisp Goody, Edmund Stedman, John King and Branwhite Oliver on 13 September 1841. This was a straight exchange, unless there was an unrecorded release the next day, 'to release and discharge from shackage and commonage certain lands within the said Borough, and for other purposes relating to other lands belonging to the said Borough'. A plan with the deeds shows that the north-western boundary coincides with the present ditch running across North Meadow from Melford Road to the Stour, with Lord Howe's land being to the west (N.M.6) and that of the late Thos Papillon Esq (N.M.7) to the south.

Three years later, on 21 August 1844, the second piece (N.M.9) of nearly four acres was conveyed in exchange for shackage by Thomas Jones and John Jones. It was bounded to the north by land owned by J. C. Gooday with the river and a drain to the west and east respectively; the plan shows that 'Places Lake' was beyond the ditch to the east; who or what Places Lake was remains a mystery.

On 7 December 1846 N.M.6 was conveyed by the Paving Commissioners of Sudbury to the Freemen for £202, again under the 1838 Act. The boundaries are described as being, on the east, lands belonging to the Corporation, e.g. N.M.5, and on land late belonging to Thomas Papillon, Esq, (N.M.7), and now to John Crisp Gooday. It appears that the Paving Commissioners had purchased these two and a half acres from the Trustees of Earl Howe's Marriage Settlement, possibly as an investment.

Records show that N.M.7, shown as two adjoining pieces, passed from Thomas Papillon's estate to John Crisp Gooday and then to Thomas Jones, for he used it as shackage redemption on 1 September 1849. N.M.8, also conveyed from Thomas Jones to redeem shackage, was obtained by the Freemen less than a year later. Thomas Jones had bought it from John Crisp Gooday, the owner in 1844 when N.M.9 was redeemed.

By far the largest conveyance of land was made on 2 September 1862. On that day Frederick Mortan, William Skipworth and John Morant ceded four parcels of land to extinguish shackage rights on receipt of £2,300. One of these meadows was Pullingford, otherwise Great Fullingpit Meadow, adjoining Little Fulling Pit; according to the deeds it contained 13 acres, 3 roods and 14 perches, an area within 0.1% of the acreage shown on the 1926 Ordnance survey used as basis for the illustration on p. 28. The other three areas were all on North Meadow (N.M.4). The acres quoted suggest that the most westerly section was known as Mill Field (5 acres 10 perches), while the area between N.M.3 and N.M.5 was known as Great Piece (12 acres and 18 perches). The smaller parcel between N.M.2 and N.M.3 was unnamed and contained 2 acres, 3 roods and 7 perches.

Perhaps one of the most interesting acquisitions was N.M.1, Colney Piece. This was originally the vineyard which, together with another field, a house and a garden, was bequeathed by John Colney, or John Colnies, as an endowment when he founded St Leonard's Hospital in 1372. He was able to use the saint's name by permission of the Archbishop of Canterbury, Simon of Sudbury. This hospital treated lepers until the 19th century when no more could be found. It carried on treating the poor for various skin disorders in the three small houses about a garden until it was finally demolished in about 1814. The new St Leonard's 'Cottage' Hospital was not built until 1868; part of the money for this was from the Colney Charity. The value of the income from this charity diminished over the years until finally the assets were incorporated into the Sudbury Municipal Charities. The Trustees of this latter charity conveyed what was by then known as Colney Piece, in redemption for shackage, to the Freemen in January 1895. The shackage rights over twenty acres on the other side of Melford Road, marked Colne Common, the other field bequeathed by John Colney, continued to be half-yearly land for another thirty years, and was the last land in Sudbury to be redeemed, this as recently as 1925.

The final portions of North Meadow, N.M.2 and N.M.3, were not conveyed until after the Charity was formed in 1897. These two doles were used in part by George Parker Weybrew in December 1901 to redeem the shackage rights over Cross Path Field and adjoining land, in total just over twenty-two acres. The other part of the agreement was for an annual rent; this was breached after several years, but the Trustees on legal advice, took no action. Thus the exchange of nearly five acres, N.M.1, 2 and 3, plus a payment releasing Colne Common, allowed an area about the size of North Meadow, from the old Bathing

Place to Brundon Mill, to be developed for housing.

From these transactions it can be seen that had the Freemen insisted on their rights of shackage and refused to accept land in exchange, the expansion of Sudbury would have been drastically curtailed. There could have been no development along Melford Road, or between York Road and Rochester Way. Other agreements indicate that nothing could have been built north of Girling Street or west of King Street; for example Newmans Road was built on Newmans Piece, released by sale of Harp Close Meadow to the Freemen. Thus is the history of Sudbury indivisible from the story of the Meadows.

'Springfield Lodge, Sudbury', pencil sketch by Richard Gainsborough Dupont. Reproduced by kind permission of Gainsborough's House, Sudbury.
Photo by Curtis Lane & Co., Sudbury

The sketch shows Mill Hill from Freemen's Great Common, with the Mill Pool and the brick structure of the Freemen's Cattle Pound bottom right.

WHO ARE THE FREEMEN?

Who are the Freemen who have these rights and claim to be the hereditary owners of the Common Lands? The origins of the Sudbury Freemen were at least a thousand years ago, so it is impossible now to give a definitive history of their antecedents. Freemen had existed in Phoenician times, and St Paul claimed he was a free man of the City of Rome; the term, as two words or one, with or without the capital F, has been used for centuries.

Today the word 'Freemen' is associated in many people's minds with traditional civic occasions, such as the Lord Mayor's Show in London. There, the Freemen are associated into 'Companies and Guilds', a very English type of club. As members they are not only entitled to but expected to take part in public life and especially in the admininstration of the international finance industry of the Square Mile of the City.

Other cities have their Freemen, as still do a few ancient boroughs. Such authorities are wont to install as Honorary Freemen worthy citizens or bodies such as Regiments on gala occasions – Sudbury last gave the Honorary Freedom of the Borough in 1929 to General Dawes, the American Ambassador and architect of the Dawes Plan after World War One, whose ancestor was born in the town in 1620.

Ancient towns of some importance are commonly known throughout Northern Europe as 'Burg', 'Bourg' or 'Borough'. Sudbury was known as Suth-burh in 798, the southern fortified settlement of the East Anglians facing the East Saxons across the river. As a garrison town it had discipline and good order, factors that attracted market traders of various types and, ultimately, financiers of such international trades as the export of wool and cloth to Flanders via Colchester.

Being relatively wealthy, due to its stability and subsequent trade, it was a good source of revenue for the overlord, be he the king, lord of the manor, or an ecclesiastical establishment. Under such circumstances the overlord could issue a charter (for a price) to say that the town was henceforth 'free' (licensed) to hold regular markets.

Such a contract had to be between responsible persons or bodies, and a grouping of the elders (aldermen) and master craftsmen (the wealth-producing burgesses) forming a 'corporation' within the town was ideal. This body, being the *de facto* governors of the town, were 'free' of feudal territorial obligations – they were the 'freemen' and guarded their privileges. Within a burgh the citizens who were free 'burghers' (burgesses) developed an elite body of chief burgesses who were even more powerful – they provided all the aldermen and mayors for many centuries. This was the foundation of the hierarchy of mayor, aldermen and burgesses and shows the historical linkage between being a Freeman and the right to vote, an exclusive privilege they enjoyed until the 19th century. It also shows how it was that the Freemen continued to dominate local government until 1835.

The labouring class were neither admitted to this circle nor able to vote on its membership; but if they had lived for a year and a day in a market town they could claim to be free; they did not then have to live in one place and work on the land of the lord as did serfs in a feudal economy.

It is probable that the freedom could be purchased from the lord of the manor, though not all the privileges were necessarily obtained for cash; this was the case both before and after the Norman invasion. Some freedoms may have been given without payment for exemplary conduct or outstanding service to the local lord in a similar way that honours are given today.

Usually one became a Freeman in Sudbury by being the son of a Freeman born within the boundary of the Borough. Later, within more recent history, one could join these illustrious ranks in other ways. The cheapest was to become apprenticed to a Freeman, following his trade – miller, weaver, jeweller, merchant – and be eligible for registration as a Freemen in the Cocket book on satisfactorily completing one's indentures, often lasting seven years. Not all succeeded; one William Shave had his application turned down on the plea of his apprentice master that the apprenticeship had not been 'duly and truly' completed; in this case the ruling was reversed by the Court of the

King's Bench in 1810.

Non-Freemen who traded in the the Borough were required to pay a 'fine', it was two shillings (ten pence) a week in 1808; alternatively they could purchase their Freedom for fifteen guineas (£15.75); this had grown to £36.15s 0d (£36.75) by 1832. These 'fines', or taxes, produced much of the income required for running the Borough, quite fairly as it meant that those who made a living in the Borough paid towards the upkeep of the infrastructure, such as it was. Much in the way of welfare was provided by the various charities. Some Freemen paid twice as these charities were often founded by or subscribed to by the richer merchants of the town.

By no means all the Freemen were well off; the size of the third son's inheritance, for instance, could be a pittance. Thus many were decidedly poor and were supported, probably preferentially, by their peers in various ways, including the distribution of 'common money'

Each Freeman had, and still has, the right to depasture two of his cattle on the Common Land, though he had to pay a 'turning-on fee'. This charge was to cover all the maintenance, namely stock-proofing the boundaries, keeping the ditches clear, repairing the bridges and paying a ranger to oversee the cattle. This right could be sold to another or, if he merely chose not depasture his cattle or was too poor to own any, he was entitled to receive a share of 'the common money' – the profit after expenses had been deducted. This custom continues to this day – but now the Freemen choose not to depasture their own cattle but exercise their right to common money by instructing the Trustees to dispose of the grazing on their behalf.

The Common Lands were also areas where Freemen had the sole rights to fish, hawk, shoot and hunt. Other stock, at one time pigs, sheep, goats and horses, could be grazed on the lands by the Freemen.

A Freeman did not have to pay market fees even at Smithfield, or pay towards the repair of the town walls or bridges; the cost of acorns for his pigs would have been nil, and he was exempt from other tolls.

Freemen, or at least the Chief Burgesses, elected the Mayor and were the only inhabitants able to vote in elections. (Sudbury had two M.P.s right up to 1841; it was declared a rotten Borough in 1844 when it became part of the Suffolk (Western Division).

One of the privileges of the Freemen had been removed a few years before this, in 1835. That was the exclusive right to the vote, particularly in Parliamentary elections. This meant that the Freemen were no longer able to sell their Parliamentary votes to the highest bidder, an important source of income for the poorer brethren! It was then that the old Corporation was abolished and replaced by the new, elected, Town Council. This body differed from its predecessor in as much as it consisted of freely elected councillors who, because of the method of their election, were more inclined to act in the interests of the whole populace rather than just the Freemen. Like all organisations, be they Masons, Buffs, Trades Unions, clerics or employers' organisations, the Freemen had looked after their own at the expense of others. Not surprisingly the new Council was soon at loggerheads with at least the more militant Freemen.

By 1835 Sudbury must have been rather like Titti Pu in *The Mikado*; it was broke, the Town Hall was mortgaged, and their senior executive occupied the posts of Treasurer, Bailiff, High Constable and Superintendent of the Common lands, all for the princely sum of £15 a year! This situation had arisen largely because of the action brought by a Mr Purr who objected to paying his fine as a 'foreign' trader. The action resulted in the Corporation not collecting the 'foreign fines' or the money from the purchase of freedoms for several years. Another rebel was a Mr Benjamin Hills, a forebear of Mr Michael Hills, jeweller and presently Town Archivist and Chairman of Sudbury Municipal Charities.

Another facet of the duplicity of the Corporation at that time: it is doubtful if these fines were ever legal! They also hid from the ordinary Freemen the fact that they were eligible to vote for the Mayor by purporting that only Chief Burgesses were so entitled.

Then, as now, there was much in-fighting and political scoring of points between groups and individuals. The Freemen alleged that the new Council had been using 'their' money for schemes they didn't approve of, using money they were not entitled to for their own purposes, were allowing the wrong people to graze on 'their' land, cut 'their' grass to make hay and sell it, and were generally not looking after the interests of the Freemen.

As the Freemen acquired more land, through purchase and redemption, relations between them and the Council grew more strained; the Freemen recruited more members – artisans, labourers, postmen and railway porters.

As in previous centuries the Freemen had to take an oath on admission to the role. The present-day oath, based on the traditional one, is:

> You shall swear that you will be aiding and assisting unto the Town Mayor and Justices of the Town of Sudbury, for the time being, the Constables, Sergeants at Mace, and all other the Queen's Officers and Ministers of the Town, in the due execution of Justice and performance of Her Majesty's service.
>
> You shall to the utmost of your power uphold, support, maintain and defend all the good and lawful rights, privileges, customs, decrees, bylaws, orders and hereditaments of and belonging to the town, and this you shall well and truly do and perform.
>
> So help you God!

This oath of allegiance should have ensured that all Freemen were honest and upright citizens. Events proved that they were subject to the same human foibles that affect us all.

The Council eventually set up a committee *c.* 1835 to investigate the rights of the various categories of Freemen (birthright, purchase, apprenticeship) *vis à vis* the freedom of the Borough and the Common Lands. They reported back that 'in the opinion of this committee the right of participating in the proceeds of the common lands is involved in so much obscurity that we recommend the Council to apply to the proper authorities for a commission to enquire and determine who are entitled to participate in the said proceeds, and if necessary to prepare a new scheme for the administration of the common lands.' In other words, they passed the buck, and the fact that every Freeman had rights in common over the lands was not determined until the High Court judgement of 1897.

As a result of this report, an Assistant Commissioner from the Charity Commission came to Sudbury to hold a local enquiry. He ruled right away that, in law, the Common Lands were a Charity. Anything held in trust for a particular class or section of the inhabitants of any town, administered by trustees, was legally a charity. By saying this he intimated that the Mayor, Aldermen and Burgesses had been acting as Trustees on behalf of all the Freemen in respect of the lands they held. Much of the time at the enquiry was spent discussing the difference between the Freedom of the Borough and the Freedom of the Commons, a distinction that had become blurred since the dissolution of the old Corporation in 1835; no conclusion was reached on this subject.

This inquiry was followed by another held by a solicitor for the Attorney-General, a Mr Clabon. He gave no ruling about the possible two types of Freedom (of the Borough or of the Commons) but, taking into account the views of the Freemen, the only people he deemed to have any proper interest in the matter, he produced a Scheme for the Regulation and Administration of Sudbury Common Lands Charity. This Scheme, approved by the High Court, came into force in May 1897 and was in use for almost exactly ninety years, until it was superseded by the present Scheme on 14 May 1987.

A Freeman of the thirteenth century, when Richard de Clare 'gave' the first of the present Common Lands to the Freemen of Sudbury (after Grimwood and Kay)

THE COMMON LANDS BECOME A CHARITY

The 1897 Scheme changed the old order. The Town Council were no longer even the titular owners of the Common Lands, the title being vested in the Official Custodian of Charity Lands with the administration in the hands of a new body, the Sudbury Common Lands Charity. The Council, as such, have had no responsibility for or jurisdiction over the Common Lands since that date.

The new controlling body consisted of the existing Trustees of Sudbury Municipal Charities (ex-officio Trustees) plus two Freemen appointed at the quinquennial meeting of the Sudbury Freemen (Representative Trustees). The Trustees of the Municipal Charity totalled twelve, six appointed by, but not necessarily members of, the Town Council and six further competent persons. Two of these were originally appointed by the Hospital Committee, two by Sudbury Board of Guardians and two by a charitable body no longer functioning in 1897, though nowadays these six are co-opted by the sitting Trustees.

The Scheme specified that the land was to be held 'in trust for the Freemen for the time being of Sudbury, according to the provisions of this Scheme'. Beneficiaries were specified as 'the Freemen who are for the time being on the Freemen's Roll of the Borough kept by the Town Clerk, as provided by the Municipal Acts, the Widows of such Freemen, including those who do not reside in the Borough.'

It also specified in writing, possibly for the first time in a legal document, that 'Each Freeman is entitled to depasture two beasts on the lands of the Charity during the year, and each Widow is entitled to depasture one beast on such lands during the year, each Freeman and Widow paying to the Trustees such sum per beast as shall be fixed from time to time by the Trustees.' Para 35 of the scheme goes on to say, 'The balance of money received in any year, after paying for officers, rates and management, shall be divided among the Freemen

In the High Court of Justice
Chancery Division
Mr Justice Romer
at Chambers

1895 A 930

Thursday the 6th day of May 1897

Mr Turner
Regr. 59

Between Her Majesty's Attorney General
Plaintiff

The Mayor Aldermen and Burgesses of the Borough of Sudbury in the County of Suffolk
Defendants

Chancery Registrars office
Entered
3. Jun 97
P. E. Reeve
Clerk of Entries

Upon the application of the Plaintiff by Summons dated the 29th April 1897 and upon hearing the Solicitors for the Applicant and for the Defendants and upon reading an Order dated the 7th November 1895 and an Office Copy Scheme filed the 9th March 1897.

And the Judge being of Opinion that the said Scheme is a fit and proper Scheme for the future management and regulation of the Charity known as "The Sudbury Common Lands Charity" Doth Order that the same be carried into effect

And it is Ordered that the lands of the said Charity do vest in the Official Trustee of Charity Lands in trust for the said Charity

And it is Ordered that it be referred to the Taxing Master to tax as between Solicitor

The first page of the High Court Judgement of 1897, creating the Sudbury Common Lands Charity

and Widows who have not depastured any beasts during the year, and who have not sold or parted with their right to do so, so that each Freeman shall be entitled to twice the amount to be paid to each Widow'.

This money was referred to as 'Common Money', a phrase unfamiliar to the ex-officio Trustees, as well as the Charity Commission, by the time 1986 came round. The fact that the Freemen had agreed in 1944 that the Trustees be empowered to let the grazing on their behalf was something that most of the Trustees were unaware of in 1986.

By the end of the first quarter of this century few Freemen depastured their own cattle. Most entered into individual agreements with one or other of the dairies who purchased their right for the year. This custom ran into difficulties towards the end of the second Great War, with so many of the Freemen away on active service, that the Freemen resolved to ask the Trustees to act as their agents. The Trustees received the money from the graziers, deducted expenses, then paid each Freeman and each Widow their entitlement. This happened for the next forty years.

The right of Freemen to the land was challenged under the Commons Registration Act of 1965. A resident attempted to have North Meadow, Freemen's Great and Little Commons, Kings Marsh and Fulling Pit Meadows registered as Town Greens, places where many villages have their football pitch and maypole. Two hearings, in 1974 and 1975, resulted in these applications being rejected, and the lands were registered as Common Land, with the rights of the Freemen to depasture cattle upheld and confirmed. No rights for other citizens were registered under this, or any other, legislation.

An application to register Harp Close Meadow as a Town Green was not made until 1991, several years after it had been sold to the Health Authority for building a much-needed hospital to replace the old Poor Law Workhouse and the out-dated St Leonard's Hospital. The County Council, who had by then been given the responsibility for this task, refused registration. The action proceeded to the High Court and then to an Appeal which was refused.

HARP CLOSE MEADOW

The circumstances surrounding this piece of land deserve special mention. As described earlier, Harp Close Meadow was bought in two pieces to provide some high-level grazing for times when the water meadows were flooded. The vendors acted under the Sudbury Town Lands Act of 1838, allowing them to provide land to the Freemen in exchange for the Freemen not grazing their cattle on other land the farmers owned. Thus the land was obtained under the same ordinance as North Meadow, along with the same rights and privileges.

By the end of the second Great War individual Freemen had ceased to graze their cattle on the lands, and graziers were paying the Common Lands Trustees for the right to depasture cattle thereon. The length of the surrounding hedge, and the fact that local residents frequently made gaps through it to gain access, meant that the cost of maintenance exceeded the rent obtained; in other words, it was a net loss to the funds of the Charity, and the Charity in those days was quite impoverished. All the surrounding land was sold by farmers for building purposes and this area was retained by the Trustees as grazing land far longer than it was needed.

As far back as December 1944 a letter was received from one Robert Pettit, Town Clerk to the Borough of Sudbury, enquiring if the Borough could purchase the land for building post-war houses. The Trustees were in favour of this, but the Charity Commission refused permission; no provision had been made to replace the land over which the Freemen still had rights.

A document written by a Mr Peter Blackwell, Surveyor to the Borough, in 1961 regarding the acquisition of the land by the Town pointed out that the only way the Council could afford to do this was by using two-thirds of the land to build houses on, and leaving the rest as a public amenity area. These sentiments were strangely echoed by the Trustees in 1984.

Attempts by the Town Council to lease or buy the land for building, recreation, or both continued until 1974. At all times the Council seemed satisfied that the Trustees had the power to dispose of the land for these purposes and that the land was not used by the Charity as a public recreational area.

To reduce the financial strain the Meadow was causing to the Charity (remember neither the Borough Council nor any other body was paying a penny towards the maintenance of what is now claimed as a priceless asset to the town), the Trustees devised ways of increasing the revenue from the field. Part of it was let at various times to the Youth Club Football Team (later to become the Wanderers Football Club), Sudbury Bambi Football Club, and Vanners and Fennell Football Club as soccer pitches; fairs, circuses and agricultural shows also rented the ground for short periods. In spite of the various efforts made by the Trustees, Harp Close Meadow remained a drain on the resources. The Trustees sanctioned each and every use; however, if the feed had already been sold to a grazier, he had the right to veto any such hirings.

Development of the land to the north-east was followed by further troubles; such items as mattresses and other household rubbish were found in the boundary ditches, causing serious flooding. This detached portion of the Freemen's land was not turning out to be the asset it was thought it would be when it was purchased; it became more and more an embarrassing millstone.

Thus it was with a certain amount of relief tinged with apprehension that the Trustees received an approach from the East Anglian Regional Health Authority in 1984 enquiring about the possibility of purchasing Harp Close Meadow as a site for a new hospital. Initially they were in favour of leasing the land with the proviso that the Health Authority lay out the area surplus to their requirements (about four and a half acres) as a public open space.

This found no favour with the Health Authority; they doubted if they could get permission for this action from the Department of Health; provision of public open spaces was way outside their remit. The Charity Commission was not enamoured with this idea either, pointing out that it was the fiduciary duty of the Trustees to take independent professional advice, to fulfil the terms of their approved scheme, and 'to obtain the best terms on a commercial footing'.

Matters proceeded slowly, with the Trustees finally agreeing that the best idea would be to sell the whole plot in one piece without any embargo on use. The Freemen also agreed, albeit reluctantly, and then only when they heard that the land might be made the subject of a compulsory purchase order.

Meanwhile the Charity Commission stated that, due to legislation since 1897, the Scheme for the Charity had become 'fatally flawed'. Their main objection was that the Charity was run solely in favour of the Freemen, a body of citizens not known to be in any special need of gratuitous largesse.

The Freemen, on the other hand, claimed that the land was theirs and that they should benefit directly from any sale; some even thought that they should divide the cash received between them while others thought that all the money should be placed in their own new charity. This charity was to be known as The Sudbury Freemen's Trust, and was being formed to commemorate the 900th aniversary of the first written record, in the Domesday Book of 1086, of the Freemen as the Burgesses of the Manor of Sudbury. The only Freemen that would be able to benefit directly from this trust would be those in need plus their families.

Richard Dunning, Clerk to the Trustees for the previous five years, produced his own ideas for reforming the Charity, the Freemen produced another, and the Charity Commissioners produced a third. They all had some things in common but on many important points there was conflict. There was also a slight breakdown in communications; the various parties used terms and precedents they were familiar with without explaining them to the other parties, e.g. 'Common Money'.

At first the Charity Commission did not recognise even the existence of this Common Money, while the ex-officio Trustees, in a parallel misapprehension, considered that the Freemen had lost the right to depasture their cattle as they had not exercised it for several years – they were unaware of the 1944 agreement where the Freemen apointed the Trustees as their agents to sell the right on their behalf!

Passions were roused. The Freemen, who once had the exclusive right to elect Members of Parliament, had been the *de facto* local government, had been historically free from many local taxes and had enjoyed extensive rights over much of the land in the Borough, found their right to Common Money, and even their right to depasture cattle, being threatened by bodies who had not studied their history!

It was not until a few representatives of the Freemen and the Trustees got together that matters were sorted out and agreement was reached. Even agreement at local level did not satisify that most powerful body, the Charity Commission. They insisted on several changes to the proposed Scheme before they would ratify it and give permission for the sale of the land to take place.

'Sudbury, as seen from the road to Charles Greenwood, Esq', by John Hawksworth after Gainsborough Dupont. Reproduced by kind permission of Gainsborough's House, Sudbury, Suffolk
Photo by Curtis Lane & Co, Sudbury

View of the Mill (left centre) from part way up Sandy Lane. The windmills on the far left of the picture are at the top end of North Street.

THE PRESENT SCHEME FOR THE CHARITY

The new Scheme differed from that of 1897 in several important respects.
- (a) The assets of the Charity were no longer held in trust *on behalf of the Freemen*.
- (b) The Freemen Trustees, previously known as Representative Trustees, were henceforth to be known as Nominative Trustees. The Charity Commissioners maintained that all Trustees, however appointed, owed allegiance only to the Charity; it was not part of their duties to make representations on behalf of their appointing body, as the words 'Representative Trustees' might indicate. Their number was doubled from two to four.
- (c) The Trustees were given permission to sell Harp Close Meadow for £850,000 as long as the purchaser paid all the costs and the total proceeds were paid over for investment in trust for the Charity.
- (d) The Trustees were allowed to purchase any land or building for the benefit of the inhabitants of Sudbury. It was this clause that allowed the Charity to buy the empty Christopher pub and permit it to be used by the Volunteer Centre as a nucleus for charitable groups.
- (e) One clause states that 'The Trustees shall manage any grazing land so as to protect and preserve it in its natural state as grazing land for the general benefit of the inhabitants of the Town of Sudbury'. This section allowed the Trustees to rehabilitate Walters and Guilford Meadows and permitted them to provide a ranger service for Friars Meadow, The Croft, Mill Acre, the Mill Lade Walk etc.

Clauses (d) and (e) talk about 'benefiting the inhabitants of Sudbury'. Like amenities provided from other sources – the library, churches, swimming-pool, toilets, bus station etc – it does not give the populace unrestricted rights to act thereon as they wish or when they please.

THE PRESENT SCHEME FOR THE CHARITY

(f) The acceptance that there could be women Freemen and that the rights enjoyed by the widows of Freemen were also available to widowers. This included the right to be considered for financial assistance in the event of old age, sickness and financial need.

(g) The Sudbury Freemen's Trust would be entitled to a quarter of the net income, after all expenses, from the investments to be held in the name of the Charity. The objects of this new Trust do not duplicate those of the Common Lands, but deal with matters of traditional interest to the Freemen. For instance, as new Freemen, at one stage, had to present two leather fire buckets to the Corporation on induction, so the present Freemen's Trust gives grants to various bodies to assist with the costs of necessary fire precautions. They also assist with the Council regalia and other civic accoutrements as well as helping Freemen in need.

(h) Grants from disposable income would be made to Sudbury Municipal Charities, to bring its diminishing income into line with its commitments, and could be made to organisations for any charitable purposes for the general benefit of the inhabitants of Sudbury, but must NOT be used to reduce rates, taxes or other public funds.

(i) The final clause states: 'Any question as to the construction of this Scheme or as to the regularity or the validity of any acts done or about to be done under this Scheme shall be determined by the Commissioners upon such application made to them for the purpose as they think sufficient.' Thus the Commissioners seem to be the only people who are in a position to rule on the validity of the sale of Harp Close Meadow to the Hospital Authority to build a hospital, and they have as much authority as the High Court in these matters. It seems strange that the protestors to the building of the hospital have not followed this route and challenged the Charity Commission.

ACTIVITIES ON THE COMMON LANDS

Rules and regulations govern life on the Common Lands just as much as they do elsewhere. In the early days most of the rules were laid down by the 'Court of Orders and Decrees' and were concerned with such items as the duties of the Ranger, the date that cattle could be turned on and the turning-on fee. Other (Council) orders concerned the activities of non-Freemen.

In 1719 an order from the Corporation that 'the footpaths leading from Ralph finches Yard to Marsh Bridge and Marsh Style be put by & that all trespassers going in the said paths (except the freemen of this Town) be psecuted at the Charge of this Corporation'.

Games had never been played as of right on the Commons. In 1764 the Council 'Ordered that the Crier give Notice that no person play at Crickett Coyts or other Games on the Comon Lands or walk thereon only on the Common path on pain of being prosecuted at the Expence of this Corporation'. In spite of this, in 1865 a cricket match was arranged on the Common and the Freemen felt constrained to lie down on the pitch to prevent its proceeding; this brought them condemnation from the Mayor. In retaliation two Freemen turned their cattle on to this area of land, spoiling the grass the Council had set aside for cutting and subsequent sale.

Not all was doom and gloom. One of the earliest rulings made under the 1897 Scheme (when the Common Lands were ruled to be Charity) was that the ranger could flood North Meadows in time of frost to allow skating to take place safely. Skating did not harm the grass; in 1902 the Ranger was instructed to warn off boys playing cricket, which he did, and the next year he was instructed to place a notice in the park, 'Trespassers will be Prosecuted'.

The grass growing on the Common Lands, like grass growing on farm pasture, is the only crop the land produces and has a cash value – in the past it was frequently sold by auction when there was a surplus.

To give some idea of what it was worth: in 1898 the grass on North Meadow was sold for £52 and in 1916 the grass that was cut before the cattle were turned on to 26 acres fetched £65. Spoiling the grass was, and is, an offence – two boys were prosecuted in 1918 for damaging the grass on Harp Close Meadow. Frequently the successful bidders for the crop were required to cut the grass after April and remove it by the end of August – they were allowed to stack it on the land at their own risk, and sometimes for a full year.

The Trustees realised that children used the meadows for play, even though they had no right to do so; they realised, too, that they often had nowhere else to go for their games. The Trustees often turned a blind eye to minor transgressions. However, the requirement to produce good grazing always took precedence; the Trust Scheme required the Trustees to manage the land for the benefit of the Freemen. The Trustees had no option – they had to ensure that the meadows produced the grass for the cattle to graze.

Thus it was that in 1906 North Street School's request for permission to play football on the Meadows was refused. This situation was echoed in 1930 when Stanley Fitch, the Headmaster of the Council School, was asked to bring to the notice of his boys that damage to the growing grass by playing football would render the offenders liable to prosecution. At the same time a notice was inserted in the *Free Press* threatening prosecution of anyone damaging the growing grass by playing football, damaging the gates or fences, or making gaps through the hedge.

In 1907 the police were asked to caution boys playing football on the Park (see below). This was followed in 1909 by the Trustees' ruling that 'Football be forbidden on all Meadows from 15th March to 29th of September and cricket be allowed after Meadows have been once fed off. No games to be played on the Park without special permission of the Trustees'. This was modified in 1913 to allow games, but not football, to be played on specified fields after they had been fed off.

It was this sort of pressure on the historic sites which led the Trustees in the 1960s to let, and then sell, to the Borough the whole of Friars Meadow for sporting activities.

'The Park', 'People's Park', or whatever other name Harp Close Meadow was known by, was the area the Trustees most frequently allowed to be used for recreation. This site was appropriate for a variety of reasons – it was self-contained and isolated from the other meadows, of a suitable size for most activities, and it was away from the river. Statistics show that, over the last fifty years, more people have been killed on the water meadows than on the roads of Sudbury! Playing near rivers and ditches, however shallow, is not a safe activity.

The legal activities of the Freemen, apart from depasturing their cattle and sharing with the public the joy of walking the footpaths, included hunting, shooting and hawking – all now forbidden – as well as fishing. It was fishing which caused most of the disputes, particularly over the use of nets. Finally in 1874 the Council ruled that the Freemen had a right to angle and that they would support that right, but would do their utmost to prevent the wholesale destruction of fish by netting. No other citizens had the right to angle for fish; and that, essentially, is the position now. Today the Trustees have an agreement with the local angling club, which is reviewed each year, that allows club members to fish if they have a rod licence, without further charge, in exchange for the club's providing bailiffs to uphold the piscatorial rights of the Freemen and the Charity.

One noteworthy dispute involving the meadows was between the Freemen and a grazier who happened to be a Freeman. In 1901 Alfred Berry, a Ballingdon cowkeeper, bought nine acres of Friars Meadow. After the grass had been cut as normal in July he turned his own cattle on to graze. The accepted date for turning on was 15 August, which was observed by the other Freemen, but by this time most of the grass had been fed off, not only from his land but also from the surrounding plots. The Trustees consulted the Charity Commission, but no further action was taken at the time. The same situation was repeated in 1904.

In 1905, to thwart this skulduggery, the Trustees instructed the Ranger to break the lock and turn the Freemen's cattle on to the pasture in July. Alfred Berry retaliated by gathering a gang of men to assist him in driving these cattle to his Ballingdon yard where he threatened to impound them. The Freemen turned out in equal force

ACTIVITIES ON THE COMMON LANDS

and they all met at the junction of Station Road and Friars Street, 147 cows and at least 14 irate drovers. At the end of the day the score was 138 to the Freemen and 9 to the Alfred Berry team. At the end of the week it was 14 in court, charged by the R.S.P.C.A. of cruelty; 10 fined and 4 let off. At the end of a further eighteen months it was game, set and match to the Trustees – Alfred paid £10 costs as the result of a writ and agreed to obey the rules, and there was no more early turning-on – by anybody. In spite of this setback he was castigated again in 1913, this time for drawing the staple of the gate to the Meadows. To illustrate the old adage of poacher turned gamekeeper, Allan W. Berry, well known as a local historian, has Alfred as a member of his family tree. Allan was a long serving Trustee of the Charity and was recently Chairman of the Freemen's Trust.

1902 saw one of the first recorded legal social functions on the meadows when permission was given to the Council to hold festivities on the Park (Harp Close Meadow) in celebration of the Coronation of Edward VII. Nine years later, in June 1911, the Trustees gave the Mayor permission to hold a pageant on Kings Marsh and Freemen's Little Common to celebrate the Coronation of King George V. Fittingly, the first scene depicted the presentation of the Charter granted by Richard de Clare giving Portmannescroft and Kingsmere to the Freemen!

Many other activities have been held on the Common Lands by permission of the Trustees.

Harp Close Meadow has seen at least three football clubs using it on a regular basis. It has also been used for fairs, circuses (but only once, as the smell of the big cats 'spooked' the cows when they returned), agricultural shows, cycling, the Territorial Army for drilling and camping, hockey, galas, the Wickhambrook Colt Show, Council Schools Sports Day, Junior Imperial League, celebrations for King George V's Silver Jubilee, the Divisional Labour Party, a Traction Engine rally, etc.

The other meadows have been used less extensively, though at one time, from 1930 to 1936, the Council leased four and a half acres of Freemen's Little Common as a sports field; the lease was not renewed

ACTIVITIES ON THE COMMON LANDS

due to its being left in an unsatisfactory state.

Part of North Meadow was let in 1935 to Sir Allan Cobham for an air display. The public could have a joy ride for 10/- (50p) and watch the Flying Flea buzzing round the sky for free from Melford Road. During the war an Air Raid Wardens' post was constructed on North Meadow near the Melford Road entrance, and in 1968 an Old Tyme Ralley was held there. In 1971 a marquee was erected on the other side of the ditch to the garden of a resident in Melford Road for his daughter's wedding breakfast, with permission, though in the same year a request to build an old people's home on the corner of North Meadow did not succeed.

'Sudbury, Ballington Bridge', from a postcard in possession of Mr Adrian Walters.

The view shows the old Ballingdon Bridge with the river in flood.
The site of St John's Hospital is on the extreme left of the picture.
The last of four wooden bridges on the site, it was built in 1805 in twelve weeks.
During this period the traffic used the fords on Freemen's Great Common
and across the Mill Pool.

DUTIES OF THE TRUSTEES

The High Court decision of May 1897 removed from the Council any rights they had over the Common Lands and vested the title to the lands in the Charity Commission. The locally appointed Trustees had total control of the management of the lands and the other assets of the Charity in accordance with the approved Scheme.

The Trustees' first job was to appoint a Clerk and a Manager. The post of Manager was quickly abolished and the duties taken over by a Management Committee of Trustees to oversee the Ranger and any casual labour. Over the years there have been many minor changes in the administration of the lands but essentially a similar situation exists today. The title 'Clerk' is still used to describe the secretary to the Charity. Latterly it was suggested that the name be changed to Chief Executive as it was felt the title 'Clerk' restricted access to others in an equivalent post. It was felt his peers likened his status to that of booking clerk on the railway or teller at a bank instead of Clerk to the Parish Council or Clerk to the Justices, all ancient and honourable titles. Today the posts of Clerk and Ranger have been combined to make a very busy full-time job.

The decisions that the Trustees were, and still are, called upon to make covered all aspects of land management. To harrow, to roll, or do nothing to the meadows frequently arose in the earlier days. Other methods of improving the crop were tried, including 'sweetening Kings Marsh by spreading two tons of salt on it' – this in 1888. Thistles, where the land had been disturbed, were another problem. Contractors were employed to cut them until the Trustees purchased a topper and were able to do the job 'in house'. Fences had to be mended frequently, hedges cut, ditches cleared, paths maintained and bridges repaired or replaced. The costs were frequently shared; for instance, in 1888 they agreed to share the cost of repairing Croft bridge, built in 1795 for the express purpose of allowing the cattle of the Freemen passage on to Fulling Pit Meadow, with the Council – the same bridge that was replaced in 1988 – and the next year had to negotiate with the miller, Mr Clover, about improving the footpath from the Croft to the Bathing Place.

The turning-on of the cattle required detailed organisation. A date was fixed according to the amount of the feed and state of the meadow; it was often towards the end of April. The Freemen would drive their cattle through the town from their winter quarters to the entrance to Kings Marsh by the old pumping station. The Mayor would be there, with mace-bearers, and they would have to pay their 'turning-on' fee – 40/- (£2.00) in 1897 – and have their beasts inspected by the veterinary surgeon and branded with the letter 'S'. The Town Cryer would call, 'All horned cows must be tottled.' A 'tottle' was a wooden (hickory?) or iron sheath tied over the horns. Later on the horns were cut short to prevent the cattle from injuring each other. Turning-on Day was quite an event for the town, and the cowkeepers took the advantage for a little socialising. The same cattle did not have to be on the pastures for the whole of the grazing season; there were specified 'change days' when the beasts could be changed, though this involved the owners in extra charges for inspection and branding.

Some Freemen were too poor to own cattle, and some did not wish to do so. Such individuals were free to sell their right of depasturing to a third party. This could be another Freeman with several head of cattle, a farmer or a dairy. In the latter case the cattle would be driven from the pasture, be it Harp Close Meadow, Friars Meadow or the Western Meadows (the meadows were fed off in rotation with cattle only returning when more fodder had grown) to the milking parlour. There were two of these in Ballingdon Street, one in Curds Lane – so named after a local family of Freemen – one in Plough Lane, another in Melford Road plus one in East Street. This practice continued until 1952 when the Trustees banned dairy cows from the meadows and the time arrived when cows and traffic could no longer share the highway. Milking cows on private land continued to be driven along some roads in the town until 1971 when Braybrookes started to 'buy in' milk rather than keep their own herd.

The Trustees would try to assess the amount of feed on the land early in the year and the cattle would be allocated to specific pastures in accordance with the number of head to be grazed. If there was likely to be a surplus of grass some meadows would be cut early for hay and grazed later. The crop was subsequently sold by auction and the proceeds would go into the funds which, after the deduction of expenses, were distributed to the qualifying Freemen.

Gradually the situation changed. From the days when the majority of Freemen owned cattle the time came when few did so. Cow-keepers were less interested in negotiating with individuals. In 1944, with so many Freemen away at the war, those remaining requested the Trustees to sell the rights on their behalf; this continued for the next 40 years and in 1987, with the sale of Harp Close Meadow, a new agreement was reached. The mixture of horses and cattle had given way to milking herds; now it is only bullocks fattening for the beef market that graze the Meadows.

Land management and supervision and control of the stock occupied most of the Trustees' time until 1945. It was then that the

Floodgate keeper's cottage, with the old Bathing Place behind the line of trees to the right, pictured in the early part of this century. It was demolished after the second World War. From a postcard in possession of Mr Adrian Walters.

Borough Council, as it then was, first approached the Trustees to buy Harp Close Meadow for post-war housing. The Trustees were in favour of selling this loss-making plot, but were prevented from doing so by the Charity Commission unless the Freemen retained the right to graze their cattle there – this precluded houses being built!

Approaches from the Council, in one form or another, continued for thirty years. The Minutes show that the Trustees were usually in favour of renting or selling if a price could be agreed, but all the proposals foundered for one reason or another. The Charity Commission ruled that the land could not be sold or leased for less than its market value. An approach was made by the Regional Health Authority in 1984. This deal was eventually successfully completed in 1987 and led to a new Scheme for the Charity; this opened the way for its subsequent role as a grant-making body.

Since then much time has been spent in committee looking after the investments and determining which charitable bodies and individuals would benefit most from financial support.

By no means all the efforts have been spent on this aspect of the Charity's work. Much time and energy has been directed into improving the lands held in trust. The interest in this came to the fore in 1971 when the Nature Conservancy Council requested that the Common Lands be registered as a Site of Special Scientific Interest (S.S.S.I.), though the basis of this registration was never explained to the Trustees. It was in the early days of environmental awareness and it seems as if all possible sites were registered then to prevent despoliation. They were subsequently deregistered in 1985.

This designation had afforded a degree of protection to the lands from outside interference and depredation. To counter the loss of safeguards resulting from deregistration the Trustees supported Babergh District Council in its application to have the meadows designated as a Local Nature Reserve. This was accomplished in 1990 with the bye-laws being approved in 1992. In 1987 the lands were also included in Suffolk River Valleys Environmentally Sensitive Area which provided further protection for the land. The regulations governing activities on the meadows by the L.N.R. designation are by no means draconian; essentially they strengthen the powers of the Trustees in dealing with cases of vandalism or misuse. Examples that have occurred that can now be more effectively dealt with include using the paths as cycle tracks, for motor-cycle testing, shooting rabbits, ducks and other wild birds, or digging holes, either as a result of using a metal detector or for collecting wild flowers.

The Trustees had been involved in conservation matters before this date. In 1953 they considered planting poplars next to Brundon Lane in celebration of the Coronation of Queen Elizabeth II but did nothing until prompted in 1957 by the Forestry Commission. These had matured by 1979 but there was no demand for the timber. The next burst of activity took place in 1988 when the bank of the river was planted with many different types of shrubs and trees – these are intended to give cover for wild-life and stabilise erosion of the banks. Other clumps of trees were planted to screen some of the less picturesque sights from view, e.g. behind the garages in Melford Road and Cross Street and near the old pumping station. In 1990 the Trustees contributed towards the cost of removing the overhead electricity cables on Kings Marsh and Freemen's Little Common; new cables were laid underground – previously several swans had been killed, and power supplies cut off, by these birds flying into the power lines.

The lands are also used as a memorial to people past and present. A chestnut tree was planted beside the Mill Pool in January 1982 as a memorial to Guy Cook, Honorary Clerk to the Trustees for nearly forty years. Another tree was planted in 1990 in a spinney near the entrance to Noah's Ark Lane on Freemen's Common in memory of Richard Dunning, Clerk 1982–1990. The spinney on North Meadow near Brundon Mill is in memory of Geoff Kisby, a long serving Trustee. The old bathing pool bridge is known as Wardman's Bridge (or Folly) in memory of Richard Wardman, chemist and former Chairman of the Trustees, and Berry's Ditch, flowing round Mill Acre, commemorates Dansie Berry, Freeman, Trustee and father of Allan Berry.

One couple who love the meadows had a tree planted there to

celebrate their Ruby Wedding, someone else planted a tree overlooking the floodgate pool in memory of her husband and a widower sponsored one in memory of his wife.

One of the most poignant memorials is on Mill Acre where Sudbury Round Table erected a plaque in memory of Roger Green (an active Tabler) and his wife and family who were all killed in the Yugoslavian air disaster of 1971.

Aerial view showing the narrow river upstream of Ballingdon Bridge before its widening in the 1950s. Also visible is the mill stream flowing between Freemen's Great and Little Commons, crossed by the footbridge on the extreme top right. The ford was where the stream widens into a lozenge shape.

Postcard in possession of Derek Kisby, and reproduced with permission.

CHARITABLE WORKS

Since Harp Close Meadow was sold in 1987 for £850,000 just over half a million pounds has been used by Sudbury Common Lands Charity in various ways for the benefit of the citizens of Sudbury.

As a grant-making organisation the Charity makes relatively few donations to individuals or organisations. Those that are made are usually large enough to be useful to the bodies concerned. These may be for the express purpose of completing a specified project or to enable them to fulfil adequately their charitable purpose; they are rarely used as a 'primer' to get an untried scheme started. Other sums are spent directly by the Charity on such projects as improving the Common Lands as a Local Nature Reserve or reinstating neglected meadows back to grazing land and wild-life habitats. One major project of the Charity was the purchase of the Christopher, a disused public house in the centre of the town, which subsequently led to its renovation and multi-purpose use as a centre of help and care for those in need in Sudbury.

Two charities closely linked with the Common Lands Charity receive the major part of their income through the investment of the money from the sale of Harp Close Meadow. These are the ancient Sudbury Municipal Charities and the newer Sudbury Freemen's Trust.

The Sudbury Municipal Charities carry on the work of a number of small charities which have combined under one umbrella. Had they tried to remain independent they would have had to have been wound up, as the value of their bequests had diminished dramatically. The money from the Common Lands investments has enabled them to continue in their traditional roles. On Ascension Day food and clothing vouchers are distributed to senior citizens of the old Borough in St Peter's Church, and at 10 o'clock on Christmas Day the older males of the town congregate in the Town Hall to receive vouchers for clothing in lieu of the overcoats the founder of the charity originally intended. In addition to the scores of beneficiaries of these vouchers about two dozen organisations receive annual grants of £100 to £200 pounds towards their running costs. These range from ex-servicemen's clubs to toy libraries and include such bodies as the Salvation Army, British Red Cross, local wildlife trust, housing societies, support groups for the blind, disabled, arthritic, hospitals, handicapped, as well as for activities such as guides, bowls, athletics, life saving, etc. Under another ancient charity, assistance can be given to persons preparing to enter a trade or profession by providing money for books, tuition fees or travelling expenses. Up to a dozen such students are helped each year.

The Sudbury Freemen's Trust was founded in 1986 to commemorate the 900th anniversary of the first written record of the Freemen of Sudbury, in 1086, as the Burgesses of the Manor in the Domesday Book. The aims of the Trust are to assist needy Freemen and their families, to promote the training of young people, to promote charitable objects consonant with the Freeman's oath, and to serve the town and community of Sudbury. Particular emphasis has been placed on giving financial assistance to provide suitable fire precautions in communal property, eg the Christopher Centre and St Joseph's Home. This type of support is particularly apt as one of the former customs was for Freemen, on induction, to present a leather bucket for use in fighting fires in the Borough. The oath taken by Freemen states that they will aid and assist the Mayor of Sudbury in various ways. This idea is perpetuated in a literal fashion by providing the mace bearers on civic occasions and paying for the refurbishment of the civic regalia. The blue plaques on old buildings showing their historical association are provided by the Trust and the proposed international construction in Belle Vue has received its support. A grant was also made to Gainsborough's House to purchase a picture of the meadows that was offered for sale and was considered historically important.

The Common Lands Charity liaises with other charities in the town to prevent too much overlapping of aid.

Apart from the organisations mentioned above, the Common Lands Charity has made direct grants to the following groups who are either based in Sudbury or who provide services to the residents of the town:

Adult Training Centre, Air Training Corps, Athletic Club, All Saints Church, Bowls Club, The Bridge, Christ Church U.R. Church, Christopher Project, Churches Together – Mission 92, Day Service Centre, Gainsborough's House, Gt Cornard & Sudbury Marching Band, Hazel Court, Helping Hands, Hockey Club, Life Saving Club, MENCAP, Quay Theatre, Red House, Relate, River Stour Trust, Rowing Club, Rugby Club, 3rd Sudbury Scouts, St Gregory's Church, St John's Ambulance, St John's Methodist Church, St Nicholas Hospice, Swan Rescue, Tennis Club and the Wanderers F.C.

*The Christopher Centre (1996), Gainsborough Street, Sudbury.
From an etching by Robin Drury*

WHAT OF THE FUTURE?

1997 sees the completion of the first hundred years of the Common Lands as a Charity, but the records of these pastures go back nearly a thousand years. The lands are now managed on a rolling five-year work plan but the ideas extend way beyond that period. Similarly the investments are not managed to give maximum short-term gain but to ensure the survival of the Charity as a viable enterprise for another hundred years or more. Both these ideals need to be flexible as ideas and objectives can change over the years; all the plans are adaptable to cope with such circumstances.

From 1262 until 1897 the lands were managed by the Mayor and Corporation of the Borough of Sudbury solely for the benefit of the Freemen of the town. The 1897 High Court judgement took control of these lands out of the hands of the Borough Council and vested them in the Charity Commission with locally appointed Trustees acting as managers on behalf of the Freemen. The 1987 Scheme ordered that the Charity should be managed for the benefit of the inhabitants of Sudbury. Thus the Common Lands, also previously known as the Freemen's Lands, have passed through three distinct phases of stewardship.

Through these years the condition of the meadows as grazing land has been of prime importance. From at least Saxon times, through the Norman and Elizabethan eras, right up to the 1960s the winter floods ensured a good crop of grass for the beasts to feed on. Sometimes salt was added to 'sweeten' the land; it was frequently harrowed. Nettles and thistles were cut by hand, ditches were kept clear and the fences kept in good repair. Sometimes accidents happened. In 1943 some cows escaped from Friars Meadow and invaded Nonsuch Meadow; a total of 20/- (£1) was paid to the three allotment holders who suffered loss; this was by no means the first time, or the last, that this sort of thing happened. Basic slag was applied to the part of North Meadow known as Mill Field in 1953 and the meadows were harrowed and rolled, these being but examples of the older methods of land management of the Commons.

Until 1987, when the Charity received the money from the sale of Harp Close Meadow, the meadows were often left for long periods with only the minimum maintenance – no ranger was appointed between 1967 and 1987; during this time the graziers were left to their own devices to do what they felt fit. In 1986 it was brought to the Trustees' attention that at least one grazier had been spreading fertilizer to increase the amount of feed; it was suspected that weedkillers had also been used. This was in direct contravention of the regulations regarding Sites of Special Scientific Interest and against the principles for registration of the lands as an area for wildlife preservation. The trouble with applied fertilisers, as with the floodwater contaminated with nitrates and phosphates, is that they encourage the growth of coarse grasses to the detriment of the more traditional mix of grasses and broadleaved plants. Since the Trustees have had the services of a Ranger to work on the meadows there has been no repetition of this.

It was the same year, 1987, that the Trustees adopted the Nature Conservancy Council's management plan for the preservation of the meadows and by the next year they had planted hundreds of trees and shrubs along the riverside of Freemen's Great Common. The following year the Trustees entered the land into the Ministry of Agriculture's Enviromentally Sensitive Area scheme; this is designed to protect wildlife habitats and traditional agricultural landscapes. Partly as a result of these steps Babergh District Council, with the active support of the Trustees, declared the Common Lands a Local Nature Reserve in 1990. This brief summary shows how the emphasis has changed from a purely agricultural approach to a conservation-orientated management programme.

It was in 1987, too, that the new Five Year Management Committee met and decided to cut down the trees in the copse on the north bank of the river on North Meadow near Brundon Mill as they were nearing the end of their natural life. This was an evening meeting – when they awoke next morning nature had taken a hand – it was the night of the 'great storm' – and virtually all the trees had been blown down. This area was cleared and replanted and named 'The Geoff Kisby Spinney' in memory of a long-serving Trustee, ex-mayor and grocer extraordinary.

What were the problems, and how did they arise, that faced the Trustees? Mainly it was a question of neglect, though there was a small amount of mismanagement involved. The drains were silted up, some of the trees were in a dangerous condition and the woodland areas overgrown with scrub. The whole area was drying out; ditches had been dug in the past to drain the wet areas, in contrast to the present policy which is to preserve them as wetlands or, possibly, 'damplands'.

In the past the main consideration has been to maximise the crop by sound farming practices. The application of basic slag, a by-product of the steel industry, added phosphates and lime to the land. Pure lime was also used by itself; both products were to sweeten the soil and encourage grass growth to ensure the largest possible hay crop for winter feed, and to give as much grazing as possible. Salt had been added too, probably as a pesticide to control soil borne pests such as crane fly and wireworm. These additions, however, were infrequent and would not have had the detrimental effect on the flora that modern fertilisers and pesticides have. The application of nitrogen to natural grassland leads to a rapid loss of floristic interest and most broad-leaved plants tend to disappear very quickly.

The major river engineering works of the 1950s and 1960s, designed to avoid the type of flooding experienced in Ballingdon in 1947 when the roads were flooded to a depth of three feet, was the cause of the meadows drying out. This, coupled with a lack of adequate management, caused a loss of wetland plants and an infestation of creeping thistle. Incidentally it was this work which caused the then Clerk to state that there was no longer any need for upland grazing as the meadows were rarely flooded during the grazing season – Harp Close Meadow was redundant from 1960!

Traces of old ditches can be seen across various pastures; some of these have been restored to irrigate the land and fresh ponds have been made to create a habitat for a range of creatures from dragonflies to frogs as well as flora such as reeds and sedges.

Generally speaking, people and wildlife do not mix well – both are scared by the presence of the other. Hissing swans, slithering snakes, and scuttling water rats are not everyone's idea of a quiet walk in the country. The meadows are, however, the home of these creatures and they are not at all like those described in the *The Wind in the Willows* or *Watership Down* or, notably, pictured by Mr Walt Disney. The animals are wild with everything that word implies. The only exceptions are the ducks which have become dependent on humans in the area round the Croft and the Mill Hotel. Here the understandable actions of people feeding them with bread has caused the drakes greatly to outnumber the ducks. Unfortunately this leads to a large number of the females being drowned by the more belligerent males, a situation the Trustees are powerless to control under the Wildlife Preservation Acts; they can only sit back and watch this unatural situation develop as any remedial action would lay them open to prosecution by the R.S.P.B.!

Elsewhere all the birds, the swans, the geese, the comorants, the kingfishers, all are wild. It is not the intention of the Trustees to provide gravel paths between enclosures so the curious can view the indigenous inhabitants from behind screens and fences as they do at Slimbridge and similar wildlife parks; the meadows are still primarily for grazing, with the conservation work an added bonus made possible by the sale of Harp Close Meadow.

Unlike films or building development, nature cannot be changed in an instant. It can take years for a few saplings to grow into a wood, for cuttings to form shrubs, for ditches and ponds to become established and for lost vegetation to recolonise. When these are in place the animals will have a chance to return. One success to date is lady's smock, or cuckoo flower, so called because it is said to flower when the first cuckoo is heard in the spring. This can be found over much of the Western Meadows and in more abundance behind the railway station on Friars Meadow. The seed pods are a favourite food of the orange-tipped butterfly's caterpillars, so it is expected that the population of this dancing flyer will increase in the near future.

Other successes so far include flowering rush and tubular water dropwort which grace some of the waterways. The ponds and ditches teem with tadpoles and frogs and as a result grass snakes are on the increase. The harvest mouse has been tempted back by leaving areas of rank vegetation adjacent to some water courses and the return of reed sweet grass and common reed (which isn't all that common) has been hastened by fencing off areas to prevent the cattle chewing them to bits.

The now rare water shrew is present and these meadows hold the only significant breeding colony of water voles in the immediate area. Some birds, too, are finding the improved environment to their liking. In 1995 kingfishers nested successfully (though secretly) and the attractive grey wagtails reared several broods.

The fenced-off areas of shrubs by the river banks provide a suitable habitat for mice and voles; these support nearby breeding tawny owls and kestrels while the bushes themselves provide suitable nesting sites for a variety of small birds. The seeding thistles in the Geoff Kisby Spinney provide food for many seed eaters including goldfinches.

It will take time to overcome the drying out caused by the work on the river and for the effect of all the unwanted nitrates and phosphates to become a thing of the past, but the hard work of the last ten years is showing fruit. The degree of this success is measured against a 'base line' obtained by a botanical survey conducted by the Ranger and a team of volunteers from Suffolk Wildlife Trust in 1991/2.

Now that the pressure is off to maximise the grass crop, the methods used on the Common Lands can more nearly approximate farming practices of centuries ago. Once the plants have reappeared they can be managed so they do not die out again, once they are established the insects will move in, then the birds and small mammals that feed off them, and so on up the food chain. The aim of the management scheme is to give nature a chance to do, in its own sweet time, what we want it to do. Nature cannot be tamed, for if it is, it ceases to be *natural* nature; but nature can be guided. On the other hand, nature cannot be left to take its own course in the prevailing conditions; much of the area would soon become an overgrown wilderness.

The Management Committee has divided the land up into areas of varying sizes to provide differing habitats; the grazing area for the cattle, the buttercups and lady's smock, the wetlands for reeds and frogs, the woodlands for the larger species, bushes for the smaller vertibrates and birds, and the river and ditches for reeds, lilies and associated aquatic life.

Having said earlier that humans and wildlife do not make a very good mix, provision has been made for much of the area to be accessible to the general public, though some sensitive areas remain restricted. Special gates allowing wheel chairs on to portions of the meadows have been constructed to the specification of the Management Committee – these have been copied at other venues, such as Flatford Mill. Unfortunately, a small minority of people seem intent on spoiling these efforts by leaving litter wherever they go, strewing picnic areas with discarded paraphernalia from take-away meals or drug-taking parties, tearing branches off young trees and bushes and stealing swans' eggs. Other thoughtless individuals kill or injure the swans by leaving nylon lines and hooks on the river banks, break down fences, often when a squeeze-gate is nearby, so letting cattle stray, or trample over special areas where rare flowers grow, or allow their dogs to worry the cattle. Kite flying is banned on the meadows for the very good reason that they frighten away food sources of kestrels and tawney owls. They also frighten cattle, as one resident discovered as he was enjoying flying an aerobatic model. The buzzing stampeded the beasts and they chased him and it was more by good luck than judgement that he escaped being trampled underfoot. It is because of the irresponsible behaviour of a few individuals that this booklet is not listing areas where the kingfishers nest or the orchids grow.

Something else that has been started since the sale of Harp Close Meadow has been an educational programme. The first event was a 'Fun Day' when youngsters were introduced to the meadows by taking part in various activities. These included making bird-boxes, junior orienteering, willow-craft, pond-dipping, and listening to a story-teller. Walks, advertised in the Press, are provided for the slightly older generations; and now instruction-packs are available for the schools, with hands-on experience on site. Work parties from some of the adult education departments take place regularly. Talks about the meadows are also given to various groups of adults in halls and rooms in the surrounding area. All these activities are carried out by the Clerk/Ranger, Adrian Walters, a qualified school teacher and linguist with a Post-Graduate Diploma in Countryside Management from Birkbeck College, University of London. He is assisted in his duties as Ranger by Ian Crighton who, since starting to work for the Charity, has completed courses in Countryside Management and Aboriculture at Otley College.

On pages 70 and 71 is a map showing where interesting features may be found, from pill boxes and a special gun emplacement, the site of the floodgate-keeper's cottage, lady's smock, a comorant's perch, the remains of the bridge between the Great and Little Common, to the pond-dipping area etc.

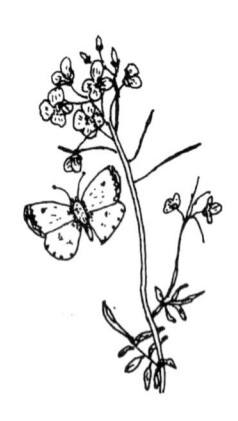

Lady's Smock, Cardamine pratensis, *also known as Cuckoo-flower and Milkmaids. Pale pink, lilac or white flowers clustered at the head of stems about 1 ft tall. It blooms when the cuckoo arrives in the spring and is food for the caterpillar of the Orange-tip butterfly.*

WHERE TO FIND WHAT AND WHEN

Winter is the quiet time on the meadows, it is the time of snow, frost and floods. However, with nature as it is, flooding can happen in September and it can snow in May. Usually things happen in order, and the following notes will tell you when you are most likely to find things of interest on the Commons.

In snow the tracks of rabbits near the railway embankment are the most obvious signs of wildlife inhabiting the area, possibly together with the footprint of a fox in pursuit of a meal; the fox may forage as far afield as the Christmas dustbin bags of houses backing on to the Common Lands, but there are no warrens on the meadows for him to patrol; rabbits do not like wet burrows.

The ducks round the Croft and the Mill together with the swans are a daily sight even in winter, with an escaped emperor goose usually in attendance. The swan cygnets will still be showing the brown of their youth, only the parents will be snow white with orange bills. The wide variety of the ducks' plumage is often confusing to the visitor, especially when a local 'expert' tells them they are Suffolk Chickens! The white Aylsburys are the easiest to identify, but they are all basically mallards who do not seem to mind breeding with various close cousins, some of whom have been dumped there by their owners. Because of the excessive feeding each duck can have two or more clutches of a dozen eggs. It is therefore fortunate that nature rules and the number of ducklings are greatly depleted by late frosts, hungry pike and other predators, otherwise the Croft would be knee-deep in feathers after a few years.

Other water birds found elsewhere on the meadows include the white faced coot and the smaller, shyer, moorhen, with the male sporting a red flash on his beak. Little grebes are dotted about the river in reasonable numbers; they are smaller than moorhens, brownish in colour, and have a rounded rump. Another usual, though fairly rare,

ITEMS OF INTEREST ON OR NEAR THE MEADOWS.

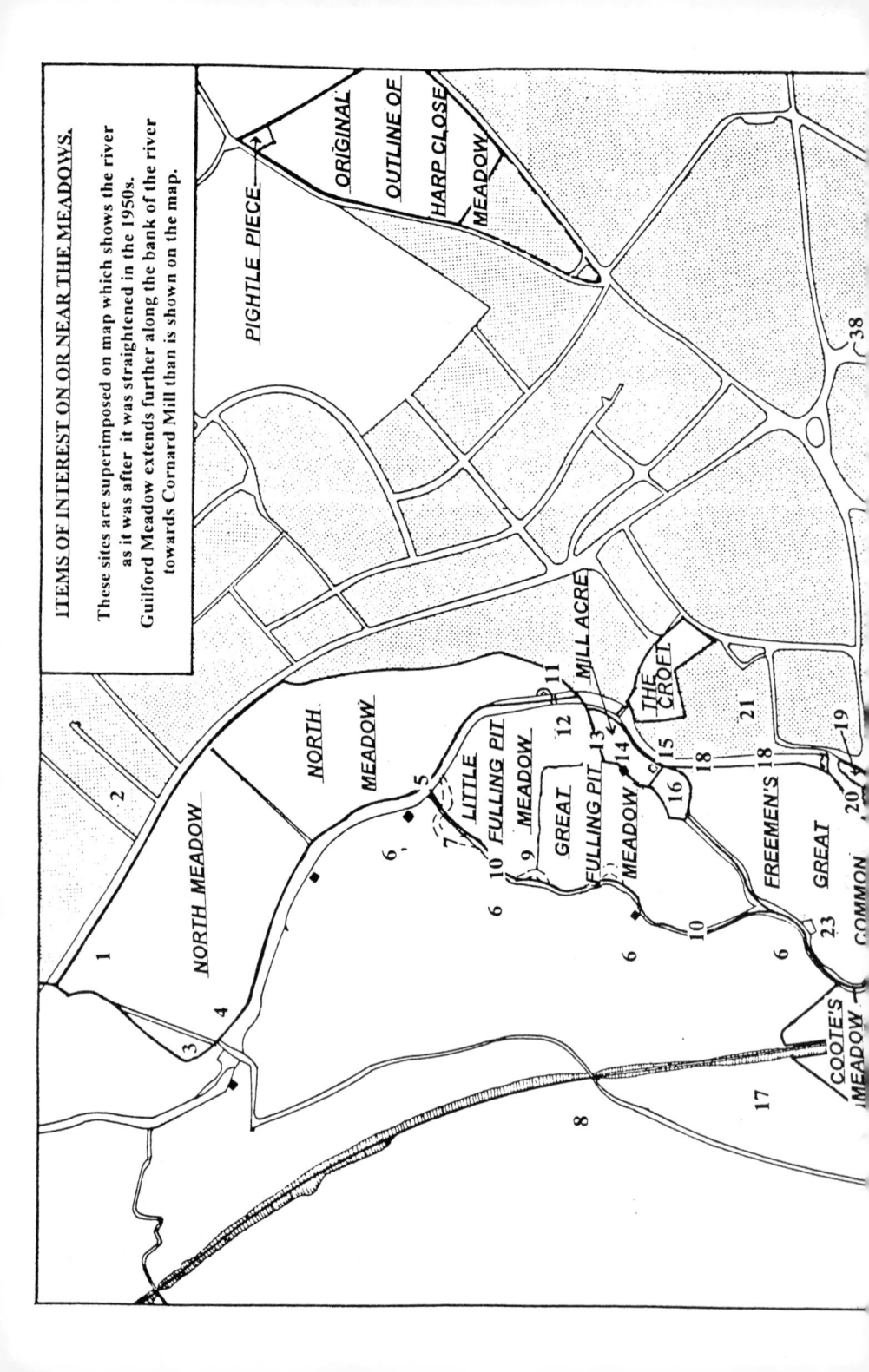

These sites are superimposed on map which shows the river as it was after it was straightened in the 1950s. Guilford Meadow extends further along the bank of the river towards Cornard Mill than is shown on the map.

PIGHTLE PIECE

ORIGINAL OUTLINE OF HARP CLOSE MEADOW

NORTH MEADOW

NORTH MEADOW

LITTLE FULLING PIT MEADOW

GREAT FULLING PIT MEADOW

MILL ACRE

THE CROFT

FREEMEN'S GREAT COMMON

COOTE'S MEADOW

- ♦ Pillboxes.
- ~~~ Old Watercourses

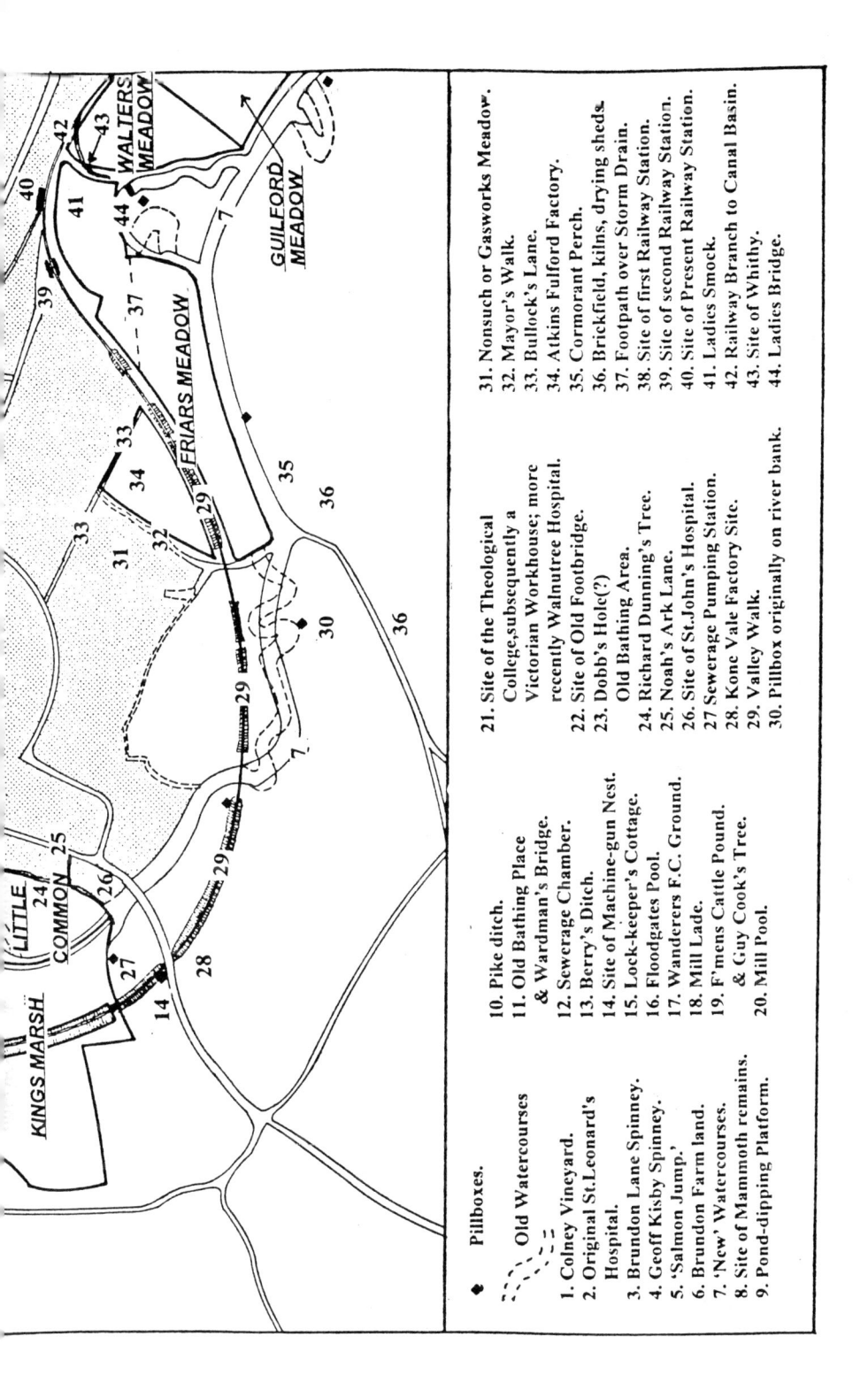

1. Colney Vineyard.
2. Original St.Leonard's Hospital.
3. Brundon Lane Spinney.
4. Geoff Kisby Spinney.
5. 'Salmon Jump.'
6. Brundon Farm land.
7. 'New' Watercourses.
8. Site of Mammoth remains.
9. Pond-dipping Platform.
10. Pike ditch.
11. Old Bathing Place & Wardman's Bridge.
12. Sewerage Chamber.
13. Berry's Ditch.
14. Site of Machine-gun Nest.
15. Lock-keeper's Cottage.
16. Floodgates Pool.
17. Wanderers F.C. Ground.
18. Mill Lade.
19. F'mens Cattle Pound. & Guy Cook's Tree.
20. Mill Pool.
21. Site of the Theological College, subsequently a Victorian Workhouse; more recently Walnutree Hospital.
22. Site of Old Footbridge.
23. Dobb's Hole(?) Old Bathing Area.
24. Richard Dunning's Tree.
25. Noah's Ark Lane.
26. Site of St.John's Hospital.
27. Sewerage Pumping Station.
28. Kone Vale Factory Site.
29. Valley Walk.
30. Pillbox originally on river bank.
31. Nonsuch or Gasworks Meadow.
32. Mayor's Walk.
33. Bullock's Lane.
34. Atkins Fulford Factory.
35. Cormorant Perch.
36. Brickfield, kilns, drying sheds.
37. Footpath over Storm Drain.
38. Site of first Railway Station.
39. Site of second Railway Station.
40. Site of Present Railway Station.
41. Ladies Smock.
42. Railway Branch to Canal Basin.
43. Site of Whithy.
44. Ladies Bridge.

resident breeding on the Common Lands is the kingfisher. These are seen over all the areas of water round the town and have been known to perch in such populated spots as Berry's Ditch and the cut just yards from the Quay Theatre. Various gulls invade from the coast and are often seen taking advantage of bread provided by the visitors.

Winter migrants often pay a visit. Kings Marsh plays host to redwings and fieldfares, while the agressive Canada geese, now considered residents in this country, are heard more often than they are seen all along the river valley.

Another resident often heard but rarely seen is the green woodpecker or yaffle, so called because of its distinctive cry. This can be heard, together with the more extended drumming of the great spotted woodpecker, in woods at Brundon, by the Mayor's Walk and along the Cornard Riverside Walk. It's worth a bit of patience to stop and look and listen and then you might catch a glimpse of these brightly coloured birds or even the lesser spotted variety which is present in small numbers.

Frosts bring another picture, with hoar-frost necklaces hanging from the trees, especially along the Mill Lade. Strange-shaped icicles hang from the sides of the floodgates while the more stagnant ditches often feeze over. This is one of the most dangerous times on the meadows – thin ice holds an almost fatal fascination for youngsters playing unsupervised. The 1897 decision to allow the Ranger to flood the meadows in times of frost for public skating is unlikely to be repeated, as the risks of litigation are too high!

Another bird difficult to see is the goldcrest, one of the tiniest European birds that cross the North Sea in large numbers. Usually found in coniferous woods they can sometimes be seen, and heard, in the scrub and bushes around the meadows. Longtailed tits are easier to spot as parties of them comb the hedges for insects.

Spring shows the Meadows in a different garb. Leaves start sprouting on the trees and bushes and catkins hang from the willows along the Mill Lade. The pigeons seem to change their call, with the first two notes mimicking the cuckoo – many an early hearing of this harbinger of spring has in fact been a pigeon woo-wooing a mate. The surest way to identify the caller in these circumstances is by its flight, more like a hawk than a pigeon.

This is the time of year for nesting, with the most obvious ones being the swans. They often build in areas frequented by people, and sometimes pay the price for this foolhardiness when their nests are raided by vandals. Ducks nest almost anywhere in the area, but the coots and moorhens find more secluded spots among the reeds.

As the cuckoo arives, so the first of the lady's smock burst into bloom. These can be found over most of the meadows, though the greatest concentration is on Friars Meadow between the railway station and Lady's Bridge, as long as the mowing contractor hasn't got there first; this should not happen in the future as the Charity is now mowing this area of the meadow 'in house' for Babergh District Council. Frogs spawn in the ditches, particularly along the Railway Walk, and in the ponds can be found newts, Caddis-fly larvae and various water beetles. A pond-dipping platform has been constructed on Little Fulling Pit Meadow just near the Pike Ditch so that schools and organised groups can learn more about aquatic life under the supervision of the Ranger and his assistant.

Arriving about this time should be the swallows and sand and house martins – swallows have the long forked tail, martins are smaller with a definite 'V' tail, and the third member of the family, the swift, has a much tighter 'V' tail and is the one that circles high in the sky in thundery summer weather. Sunny weather will also bring out the basking reptiles, slow-worms, grass snakes and the common lizard, on the new Nature Reserve of the Cornard riverside.

Brundon Lane Wood is the place to find the blossom of the wild cherry, though it is best viewed from the lane as the large clumps of comfrey, angelica and nettles form an almost impenetrable mini forest of vegetation, a good habitat for insects and small animals.

Usually in April the blackthorn is in full bloom, to be quickly followed by the hawthorn in May, all along the Valley Walk. Birdsong comes from almost every bush and tree, the blackbird and song thrush, apart from the sparrows, are the most common – the mistle thrush is more likely to be found on the pastures. Reed buntings nest in the tussocky vegetation on the river bank of Freemen's Great Common and may be seen swinging on the seedheads of the reeds.

Alderflies make their appearance at this time, the larvae having left the ditches and ponds to pupate in the damp soil, and the tadpoles have hatched from the spawn to swim in the water. With the lady's smock and garlic mustard in bloom the orange-tip butterfly makes its appearance. As is usual in nature it is the male that is the more striking; only he has the orange tips to his wings.

April 1st is the time for the cattle to be turned on to Kings Marsh. When first given the freedom to graze and roam at will the beasts are often skittish and wary of humans and dogs; it is advisable not to be too confrontational at this period. On the other meadows grazing will start in rotation, necessitating the erection of temporary fencing.

About this time of the year experts may well find the willow, sedge, and reed warblers, or even the grasshopper warbler, together with chiffchaffs and whitethroats, all summer visitors which like woody/scrub/reedy areas round the town.

June is the month when acre after acre of the meadows are dressed in buttercup yellow. The grazing cattle do not despoil this sight, in spite of the opinion of some, but rather their presence is important for the proliferation of the meadow buttercup to give a sight that used to be common in much of the countryside before the advent of chemical sprays.

Marsh marigolds and ragged robin, two species that reappeared in 1991, have taken hold on much of North Meadow from the seed bank that had lain dormant for many years. Now is the time that house martins collect the building material for their nests from the river banks and ditches where the pied wagtails feed. After a year or two living in ditches or ponds the dragonflies and damselflies start emerging from their nymphs to spend just a few weeks as a winged insect before laying their eggs, beginning yet another life cycle.

In July, specially in a dry year, the meadows lose their freshness and sparkle. This is the time the grasses flower and pollinate to ensure their succession. It is particularly fortunate that these meadows are one of the last homes for native grasses like crested dog's tail,

Yorkshire fog, meadow barley and tufted hair grass, to name but a few. Before it was fashionable to plough up the flood plain or use weedkillers and fertilizers to increase crops, such species would have been widespread on rural meadows. With the advent of the food so the insects follow, in this case the meadow brown butterflies which can be seen in their hundreds at this time of year. In Fulling Pit Ditch, round the area which was fenced off to give it a chance to multiply, is the flowering rush, surviving in spite of attacks by cattle and water voles. The previously rare black-tailed skimmers (dragonflies) also find this area attractive.

By August there should be no long grass on the Meadows; it should have all been grazed off. Over the years the activities of the cattle on the Meadows have given rise to a certain number of complaints. Some people don't accept that these are traditional grazing lands and object to the cattle being there, they find them intimidating and messy. Unless worried by dogs, frightened by kites or low-flying aircraft, or plagued by insects, the beasts are normally quite docile after they have been on the Meadows for a few days. It is admitted that care must be taken where one treads, but apart from fencing off the paths or fitting the cattle with nappies, both ideas the Trustees consider inappropriate, there is little that can be done. This ancient tradition of grazing cattle on the land, an activity which has produced the sward as it is today and is one of the main functions of the Charity, will continue.

At this time of year the centres of interest from the naturalist's point of view are the river banks. Here numerous plants are in full flower. The regal stems of purple loosestrife give a magnificent splash of colour, while clumps of hemp agrimony provide a plentiful source of nectar for the wonderful profusion of butterflies. Himalayan balsam, an escapee from Victorian greenhouses, is in flower; later it will have violently exploding seed capsules which ensures it will spread in the damp habitat. The tadpoles will have metamorphosed into frogs by this time and may sometimes be found in dryer areas trekking from one watery habitat to another. Unlike the swallows and martins the swifts do not congregate on telephone wires and will be heading south by the middle of the month.

September normally sees the end of the summer. Fulling Pit Meadow hosts cat's ear, a yellow member of the daisy family which provides nectar for hoverflies and butterflies during opening hours – the flowers close in the late afternoon. In the ditch nearby are trifid bur marigolds, so named because of their three-lobed leaves and the burs on the seeds; the flowers though are disappointing, resembling small dull yellow buttons.

Apart from the meadow browns and cabbage whites a few butterflies more usually seen in gardens venture on to the Meadows. These could include the comma, easily distinguished by the light comma on its jagged underwing, the peacock with its peacock 'eyes', red admirals with red splodges on each back wing, the tortoiseshell, and the brimstone, bright yellow, and usually the first to be seen in the spring. Though late summer/early autumn is the time that these are about in large quantities many can be seen much earlier in the year; this is known as the 'first flight' when they mate and lay their eggs which hatch into caterpillars, pupate and emerge as butterflies all in a few short months.

October heralds 'the season of mists and mellow fruitfulness', and no more so than round these meadows. Along the Valley Walk sloes are ripening purple, walnuts swelling, and soon the hawthorn will provide food for the winter visitors. At the Croft and Old Bathing Place ripe conkers drop to the ground and the grand old oaks lining the road enable the ducks to supplement their diet of (white) bread with acorns. The cygnets will be flexing their wings with circuits and bumps and the surviving ducks will have grown out of all recognition. As the mists gather the cattle leave for their winter quarters and nature changes from greens and bright yellows to rusty reds and subdued hues. Much of nature seems to doze until awoken in the spring.

Of the insects still around in autumn the dor beetle is the most conspicuous. These large lumbering black beetles can be seen on the pastures, busy burying lumps of cow dung for the larval stage of its life cycle. Look closer and you might see the red mites congregated on its body – hence the name lousy watchman.

PERMANENT FEATURES

Certain things can be seen on the Meadows at any time – the river, trees, the grass; they are there and merely change their mood throughout the year. Some things don't change very much with the seasons, particularly the man-made objects. These include the weir/salmon-jump, the floodgates and the mill with its water wheel. There are many other artifacts nearby, some old, some more recent.

One of the oldest sights is St Gregory's Church on the Croft which contains the skull of Simon of Sudbury, Lord Chancellor and Archbishop of Canterbury who was murdered by rebels in the Peasants' Revolt. Just west of this, through a gate set in a tall wall, is Walnuttree Hospital, formerly a Victorian Workhouse Infirmary known as the Union or Spike. This had been rebuilt in 1835 on the site of St Gregory's College, an ecclesiastical establishment founded by Simon of Sudbury in 1375 on land next to the family home of the Theobalds. The college was at one time the largest landowner in Sudbury, being endowed with the Manors of Ballingdon and Middleton before being dissolved in 1538.

There have been two other hospitals on the perimeter of the Common Lands. The leper hospital of St Leonards was founded by John Colney and received its charter of dedication from Simon of Sudbury in 1372 and was sited on the north side of Melford road where Colney Close now stands. St John's Hospital was in existence nearly two hundred years prior to this, just off the north-west of Ballingdon bridge. The only reminder today is a sign saying Hospital Yard and a blue plaque erected by the Freemen's society.

Other structures include the old Bathing Place just upstream from the Croft. Only the bar, denoting the edge of the shallow area, can be seen. Gone are the changing cubicles in a semicircle behind the minature bay, with the spring-boards at either side, and the instructor's kiosk. The trees have grown since it closed in 1936.

One of the newest constructions is the boating lake on Mill Acre, built in 1971, with its plaque commemorating Roger Green and his family, who lost their lives in the Yugoslavian air disaster.

Across the river to the western end of Friars Meadow, in the wood lining the old canal containing the remains of the barges sunk during the first war, are the old workings of Allen's brickfield. The remains of at least one kiln survive in the wooded area; the drying sheds were on the flat piece of ground near the junction of the canal and the river. Before the coming of the railways barges were an important form of transport. Head of navigation was Ballingdon Bridge, the quays were at the end of Quay Lane and another, with a boathouse, was used to unload coal for the gasworks and was situated where the Mayor's Walk joins Bullocks Lane. There was also a basin at the foot of Middleton Road hill where the canal passed under the road; this was used to load the bricks to be shipped to London to build the Albert Hall. The railway even built a spur towards Lady's Bridge to load and unload freight from the barges.

A group of buildings that deserve special mention are the the wartime defences erected in 1940/41 on the Sudbury/Cornard meadows. These consist of pillboxes and line the Stour, mainly on the Essex bank, from Bures to Melford. There are, or were, about three dozen in this stretch with about a third of them on or near Sudbury's water meadows. Nearly all were of the standard hexagonal type made of a concrete/brick mixture with sides up to 3'6" (1.068 m) thick, some with blast walls protecting the entrance. The more common ones had a circular opening in the roof over a thick column for the mounting of a Bren to be used as an anti-aircraft gun as well as slits for rifles round the sides. The only one on the Common Lands has been filled with gravel to prevent drug addicts and other undesirables loitering there.

There were two rare variants nearby, both now demolished. Local memories indicate that one type was situated on Mill Acre and was a 'one-man' domed metal machine-gun nest – a similar one was positioned at the top of North Street opposite the Masonic Hall with a view along Melford Road – both were manned by the Home Guard and armed with spigot mortars known as Blacker Bombards. The second type near the meadows was similar in design and known as a Tett Turret. This was a concrete structure built into the embankment on the south-western corner of the railway bridge over Ballingdon Street behind railings – it could only direct fire along the road, not over the river or meadows.

Other defensive measures were employed in the area. Firstly, all the small bridges were removed to prevent invading foot soldiers from crossing, and secondly, tall poles were erected on the meadows to prevent gliders from landing in the event of an airborne invasion. 'Dragons teeth', toothed concrete blocks, were also laid in strategic positions as tank traps. One set was the other side of the railway line from Lady's Bridge and another near Brundon Mill bridge. Firing slits were put in many structures, including the foot-bridge crossing the railway line near the Cornard end of the present rail platform.

Fortunately none of these defences was put to the test.

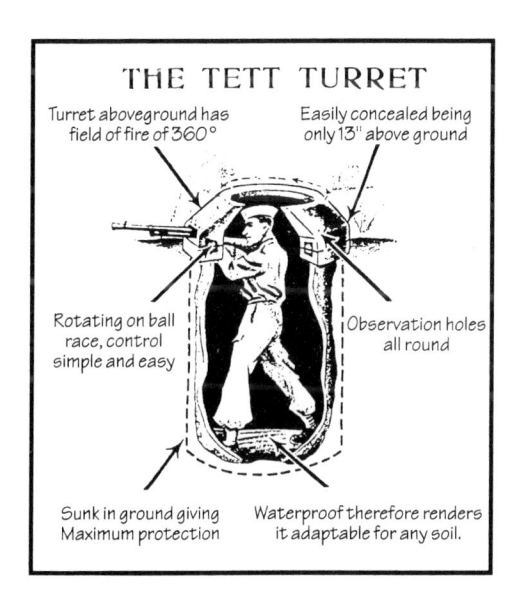

THE TETT TURRET

- Turret aboveground has field of fire of 360°
- Easily concealed being only 13" above ground
- Rotating on ball race, control simple and easy
- Observation holes all round
- Sunk in ground giving Maximum protection
- Waterproof therefore renders it adaptable for any soil.

An example of the rare one-man pillbox, the Tett Turret, at Sudbury, Suffolk.
From Henry Wills, Pillboxes: a Study of U.K Defences 1940
(Leo Cooper 1985), p. 22

POSTSCRIPT

Names of some things can be confusing, such as Common Lands, when they are not common to all, and Peoples Park when it never belonged to the town or the people and was never used as a park – no unlocked gates, no paths, no flower beds, no swings – nothing that makes a field into an urban park.

Other misleading names in Sudbury include Bullocks Lane, which suggests that it was where the bullocks were driven when going to or from Friars Meadow. Not so, it was named after a Mr Bullock who lived in Friars Street at the entrance to the lane. Nonsuch Meadow existed, despite its title; it was named after a lucern-like plant which has tiny yellow flowers and black peapods, also known as black medic, which can still be seen there on the verges of the housing estate on what was also known as Gasworks Meadow. Kone Vale, often pronounced 'Koney Vale' (Sudburians have a yen for adding an extra syllable to a name), has nothing to do with Colney Place and is on the Stour, not the Colne, and was named after a chicken-processing plant that used to occupy a site near the entrance from Ballingdon Street by the side of the old railway embankment. There are now no Black Friars in Blackfriars, or schools in School Street, friars in Friars Street, abbeys in Abbey Road or walnut trees in Walnuttree Lane. Gainsboroughs can still be found in Gainsborough Street, but only paintings. His birthplace was in Sepulchre Street, in spite of containing no tomb even in Gainsborough's day; and in 1714 Cor Brewer named it St Pulcher's Street in his map after a church of that name situated towards the junction with School Street, possibly the Anglicised version of St Pulcheria (b. 399), an Empress of the Eastern Roman Empire.

The Meadows, though, remain the Meadows, whether they are called Freemen's Meadows, Sudbury Meadows, Common Lands or just 'Our Meadows'.

Para 25.4 of the 1987 Scheme approved by the Charity Commissioners states, 'The Trustees shall manage any grazing land so as to protect and preserve it in its natural state as grazing land for the general benefit of the inhabitants of the Town of Sudbury'. Thus it is the duty of the Trustees to do all they can to see that these meadows remain as grazing lands for as long as possible, hopefully for another thousand years. Being managed by a charity formed for this express purpose, and not by a local authority or commercial undertaking, the possibility of political or financial interests influencing decisions on the management of these meadows is greatly reduced; the Trustees obligations are quite clear. This system has the added advantage that any management decisions taken can be implemented quickly without having to be refered to higher authority. Do remember that nearly all the other fields and meadows round the town that the Freemen used to graze have been sold for housing, starting with the Act of 1838, and the present Common Lands are the last open spaces of any size within the town boundary, a situation the Trustees are charged to maintain.

Certain trends, though, are worrying. Vandalism and thoughtlessness, in various forms, are on the increase, here as elsewhere. Trees and bushes are uprooted, fences breached, litter bins set on fire or dumped in the river together with shopping trolleys, trees are torched and rubbish dumped. The nests of swans are raided and the eggs smashed, fishing lines and hooks are left lying about and swans die, and certain areas are the haunts of drug addicts and become contaminated with their rubbish. It is hoped that the educational programme run by the Charity in the schools and elsewhere will help to diminish this type of anti-social behavour.

In addition, hundreds of pounds worth of damage has been caused to the Meadows by criminal acts away from the affected areas, mainly via the storm drains. There have been examples of this in many of the ditches surrounding these lands, but the drain from the Chilton Industrial Estate has given most cause for concern. Large quantities of toxic waste has flooded from there on to the grassland and only determined action has prevented the river from becoming contaminated. These incidents were due to sheer vandalism (opening valves on oil tanks and leaving them running), carelessness in disposing of industrial waste, or just plain bloody-mindedness in not following safety procedures. Anglian Water has taken steps to limit this nuisance which may or may not be successful.

On another level, but much more common, is the litter problem; drink cans, plastic bags, bottles and take-away food containers in the main, though the provision of litter bins in the more popular areas has helped. All the same, a disproportionate amount of time is spent in clearing up after these thoughtless types, especially when it is remembered that the whole of the Charity only employs one full-time Clerk/Ranger and one part-time assistant to do all the clerical duties, arrange and carry out the physical work on the Meadows, liaise with classes either in schools or on the Commons, give lectures and talks to various groups, and stage guided walks for the public.

Without putting yourselves in jeopardy, any help in stopping such anti-social behaviour would be appreciated. Such assistance would help to ensure that the Common Lands can continue to be an asset to the town of Sudbury. The epitaph for Richard Dunning, a former Clerk to the Charity, as 'one who loved these Meadows' would then be enshrined for all those who cherish this inheritance as well as their descendants.

Nonsuch, Medicago lupulina, or Black Medick. A member of the pea family, but it looks more like clover, with yellow flowers and clusters of miniature black pods.

APPENDIXES

Trustees and Officers of the Charity   84

Extracts from Minute Book circa 1902   85

The Common Lands Today   86

Comparison of Areas of Lands According to Source   87

APPENDIXES

TRUSTEES & OFFICERS OF THE CHARITY

TRUSTEES

1897	1947	1997
Edgar Mann *	Charles G. Grimwood *	John Wardman *
Christie Mauldon **	Richard W. Wardman **	Peter Scott **
W. L. Lewis	P. H. Jordan	M. Hills
B. R. Marten	C. H. Hitchcock	G. Challacombe
J. Bell	M. J. Blythe	D. Kisby
P. Constable	C. E. Grimwood	P. Richardson
M. Death	A. B. Walters	V. Waters (C)
E. J. Wright	R. J. Marshall	E. Wiles (C)
W. Nunn	C. G. Wright	J. Frankham (C)
G. P. Weybrew	S. G. Wheeler	S. Cann (C)
H. H. Baker	J. W. Bitten (F)	R. Titmus (C)
J. Alexander	J. French (F)	N. Irwin (C)
T. Sillitoe (F)		J. Nurser (F)
W. H. Wright (F)		I. Parsonson (F)
		.S. Prior (F)
		A. Wheeler (F)

*Chairman ** Vice Chairman*

(F) Denotes appointed by the Freemen. The others are Trustees of Sudbury Municipal Charities. The S.M.C. has six Trustees appointed by the Town Council (C), and six by the sitting Trustees. Prior to 1954 two had been appointed by each of three charities, namely the Hospital Committee, Sudbury Board of Guardians and a third (unknown) charity, defunct before 1897, until all these bodies ceased to exist.

CHAIRMEN

Edgar Mann (1897–1899); Christie E. Mauldon (1899–1913); G. P. Weybrew (1913–1913); H. S. Oliver (1913–1926); H. A. Hitchcock (1926–1929); G. C. Grimwood (1929–1952); P. H. Jordan (1952–1956); R. W. Wardman (1956–1971); R. C. Oliver (1971–1983); John Grimwood (1983–1986); John Wardman (1986–)

CLERKS

J. Alexander (1897–1911); T. M. Braithwaite (1911–1937); Miss D. E. Palmer (1937–1941); Guy Cook (1941–1981); Richard Dunning (1981–1990); Adrian Walters (1990–)

VETERINARY INSPECTORS

Mr Miller (1897–1899); R. E. Godbold (1899–1931); Percy Godbold (1931–1952). No appointments were made after 1952.

Barclays Bank were the bankers prior to 1897 and still are today.

APPENDIXES

EXTRACTS FROM MINUTE BOOK circa 1902.

(Identification of meadows added to original entries IN CAPITALS.)

Page 431/2.

Particulars of Lands comprised in the Trust.				
Acreage a. r. p	Description	Tithe Apport.		
16. 0. 0	Pig Tail Piece H.C.M.	Redeemed		
10. 0. 27	Part Commons F.L.C.			
		No.		
* 3. 0. 21	Colney's Land N.M.1	128	£	1. 15. 0.
65. 2. 0	Gt & Lt Fullingpit & North Meadow	151	£	8. 0.
3. 36	N.M.3.	153	£	7. 6.
3. 27	N.M.2.	"		"
3. 2. 0	N.M.5.(PART)	155	£	1. 8. 0.
2. 19	N.M.5.(PART)	156	£	5. 8.
2. 26	N.M.5.(PART)	157	£	5.10.
2. 0. 4	N.M.7	158	£	16. 6.
4. 0. 7	N.M.5.(PART) TOTALS 8.3.12.	159	£	1. 13. 6.
2. 2. 6	N.M.6.	160	£	1. 2. 0.
2. 0. 16	N.M.8.	161	£	17. 0.
3. 3. 24	N.M.9.	162	£	1. 13. 6.
10 .1. 26	L.F.P.	166	£	5. 5. 0.
			£	15.17, 6.
5. 0. 10	N.M.4. (MILL FIELD)	150		Redeemed
2. 3. 7	N.M.4.	152		"
12. 0. 18	N.M.4. (GREAT PIECE)	154		"
13. 3. 14	G.F.P	168		"
65. 2. 0				
12. 1. 23	Part Commons F.G.C		£	1. 8. 8.
19. 0. 34	Kings Marshes K.M		£	5. 6. 4.
Aftermath	Friars Meadow F.M.			

* This to be added to the acreage of North Meadow as given in the schedule to the scheme making it 44. 1. 21.

Page 433.

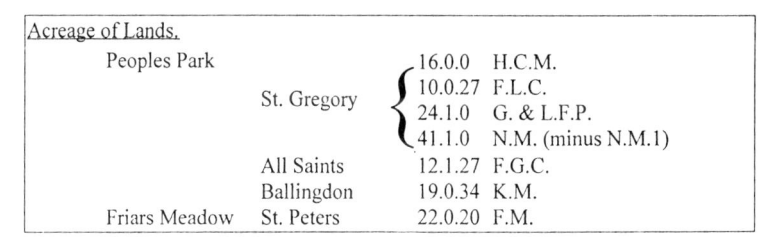

Acreage of Lands.			
Peoples Park		16.0.0	H.C.M.
	St. Gregory	10.0.27	F.L.C.
		24.1.0	G. & L.F.P.
		41.1.0	N.M. (minus N.M.1)
	All Saints	12.1.27	F.G.C.
	Ballingdon	19.0.34	K.M.
Friars Meadow	St. Peters	22.0.20	F.M.

85

THE COMMON LANDS TODAY

Map ref.	Name	Obtained from.	Date	Price	Acres
F.G.C.	Freemen's Gt Common	Richard de Clare	c1260	£5	18.0
F.L.C.	Freemen's Lt Common	Richard de Clare	c1260	plus	4.5
K.M.	Kingsmarsh	Richard de Clare	c1260	£2 pa.	19.2
N.M.1	North Meadow 1	Colney Chty(Shackage)	1895	Exch.	2.9
N.M.2/3	North Meadow 2 & 3	Weybrew (Shackage)	1901	£7.10s10p	1.9
N.M.4	North Meadow 4	Mortan, Skipworth, Morant (Woodhall Shackage)	1862*	£1,360	20.0
N.M.5	North Meadow 5	Goody, Stedman, King Oliver (Shackage)	1841	Exch.	8.7
N.M.6	North Meadow 6	Paving Commissioners	1846	£202	2.5
N.M.7	North Meadow 7	T. Jones (Shackage)	1849	Exch.	2.5
N.M.8	North Meadow 8	T. Jones (Shackage)	1850	Exch.	2.1
N.M.9	North Meadow 9	Jones (Shackage)	1844	Exch.	3.9
L.F.P.	Lt Fulling Pit (part)	John Knight	1731	5/-	8.0
L.F.P.	Lt Fulling Pit (rest)	John Taylor	??	??	2.45
G.F.P.	Great Fulling Pit	Mortan, Skipworth, Morant, (Woodhall Shackage)	1862*	£940	13.8
P.P.	Pightle Piece (1)	Argent (Shackage)	1875		0.7
H.C.M.	Harp Close Meadow (1)	Grover	1876	**£1,628	15.3
F.M.	Friars Meadow (2)	Various, last part in	1959	??	22.2
C.M.	Coote's Meadow	Armsey	1959	£125	4.7
W.M.	Walters Meadow	Stephen Walters Ltd.	1994	Leased	6.6
G.M.	Guilford Meadow	Guilford Europe	1995	Leased	12.5

Exch = Redemption of shackage without financial adjustment.
* Purchased using money from G.E.R. for sale of land for railway.
** Purchased using money for releasing shackage at Woodhall.

(1) Sold to Regional Health Authority 1987 for a new hospital.
(2) Sold in two portions, the area north of the railway line, to Atkins Fulford Ltd as a factory site in 1960 and the remainder to Sudbury Borough Council in 1965 after leasing it to them as a sports field for some years.

COMPARISON OF AREAS OF LANDS ACCORDING TO SOURCE.

	DEEDS A R P	DEEDS DECIMAL	MINUTES c1902	1897 SCHEME	1926 MAP	1987 SCHEME	1971 MAP
F.G.C.	17 3 12*#	17.825		18.020			
F.L.C	4 0 20*#	4.125		4.677			
TOTAL	21 3 32*#	21.95	22.563	22.563	22.697	22.41(i)	22.88
K.M.	21 0 36*#	21.225	19.213	19.213	19.214	14.77(i)	18.84
N.M.1	2 3 22	2.888	(3.13)	(ii)			
N.M.2&3	1 3 23*	1.894		---			
M.N.4	19 3 35	19.969					
N.M.5	8 2 37	8.731					
N.M.6	2 2 6	2.538					
N.M.7	2 2 1	2.506					
N.M.8	2 0 16	2.100					
N.M.9	3 3 24	3.900					
TOTAL	44 2 4	44.253	44.381	41.25	46.08	42.19	45.47
L.F.P	8 0 0	8.000					
L.F.P	2 1 30*	2.438*					
Total	10 1 30	10.438			10.416		
G.F.P.	13 3 14	13.838			13.862		
G.&LFP	24 1 4	24.275		24.25	24.278	22.99(i)	23.27
FP&NM	68 3 8	68.800	65.5 (68.63)**				68.74
P.P.	0 2 29	0.681				0.681	Not
H.C.M	15 1 11*	15.319*				15.319	Listed.
TOTAL	16 0 0	16.00	16.00	16.00	? ? ? ?	16.00	(16.0)
F.M.(a)(Atkins Fulford)					5.304	- -	(5.30)
F.M.(b)					16.211	- - -	15.51
TOTAL	22 0 20*	22.125*	22.125	22.125	21.515	- - -	20.81
C.M.	4 2 32*	4.700*	- - -	- -	4.675	4.68	4.68
TOTAL	*154 2 05*	*154.529*	*148.531*	*145.40*	*154.459*	*123.04*	*151.95*
W.M.		6.6		(6.6)	6.6		6.6
G.M.		12.5		(12.5)	12.5		12.5
TOTAL		**173.629**	**(172.331)**	**(164.5)**	**173.559**	**(167.77)**	**171.05**

* AREA NOT SPECIFIED IN DEEDS BUT DETERMINED BY OTHER MEANS.
*# AREA ACCORDING TO THE COR BREWER MAP OF 1714.
**INCLUDING N.M.1, COLNEY PIECE.
  (i)ERRORS IN 1987 SCHEME:- Areas on adjacent map sheets omitted, 0.47 acres on F.L.C. and 4.07 on K.M. plus cattle pound on L.F.P (0.28 acres).
  (ii)ERROR IN 1897 SCHEME (Colney Piece omitted from schedule).
  N.B. The difference between the deeds total of North Meadow and both the 1897 & 1987 schemes may be that the 2.4 acres of Brundon Lane spinney was missed; it was not included in the Kay & Grimwood book. Other variations can be accounted for by the building of the railway, the widening of Brundon Lane, the extension of Bullocks Lane and the dredging the river.